LETTERS FROM LOST PRAIRIE

LETTERS
FROM
LOST PRAIRIE

Rosemary McKinnon

Photographs by
Candace Gaudiani

LOST HORIZON

Lost Horizon | 2013
9705 Lost Prairie Rd. Marion, MT 59925

www.montanaacademy.com

ISBN 978-0-578-11556-6

CONTENTS

LETTERS FROM LOST PRAIRIE

INTRODUCTION

This week, one of the students at Montana Academy asked me what year the school was founded. I told her that we bought the Lost Trail Ranch in the Lost Prairie Valley and accepted our first students in 1997. She told me that this was the year that she was born.

The first years in the start of any new business are likely to be busy ones and that was certainly the case for the four of us who founded Montana Academy. We had not done anything like this before and did not have a clear plan about how to put such a new kind of school together. We had experience trying to treat adolescents in both in-patient and out-patient settings and were unimpressed by the results. We imagined a hybrid school with equal measures of therapy and education that would be woven together with outdoor activities in such a way that our students would experience an integration of these various parts of their lives. We hoped that all staff interactions with students would be informed by close relationships and an understanding of their individual needs. We wanted parents to be involved and knew that we would not be successful without their dedicated collaboration. But since our students came from all over the United States and sometimes from beyond its borders, we had to craft a way to involve them with their children's therapy through letters and phone calls. We held twice-a-year workshops that parents attended from far and wide and we invited them to come to the campus for visits every two or three months.

The first few years we experimented with rules and ideas about how long each student needed to stay and what it was that we thought we were trying to do. We invented the idea of "clans" to keep track of our students' progress and to carve out tasks for different phases of the program. "Clans" follow a progression skyward: Earth, Moon, Sun, Star and Sky and have different themes and curricula. Students settle in, accept treatment in Earth Clan and learn to abide by the rules. In Moon Clan they embark on a rigorous therapeutic journey of self-discovery leading to better self-control. In Sun Clan they work to understand their family and repair their relationships. In Star Clan they take on positions of leadership in the community, begin to work on future plans, practice making visits home and work out how to prevent relapses. Sky Clan is a short exercise in staying present while getting ready to say goodbye. It took a good deal of experimentation and several years of trial and error for us to settle into what appears now, more than a decade later, to be a well thought-out routine and culture that is dedicated to the task of helping young people who are struggling to grow up.

As we talked and worked with our population of bright but failing students, often alienated from their parents and rapidly throwing away their gifts and opportunities for engaged and fulfilling adult relationships and lives, we came to realize that behind the veneer of unhappiness and flailing these handsome young adolescents were, in fact, exhibiting the behavior of much younger children. They were caught in earlier stages of development where they had difficulty imagining a world beyond themselves and so lied and cheated with little remorse, treating their parents with angry contempt and failing to see any connection between the present and the future. In short, beyond the symptoms, we realized that we were dealing with questions of character and the failure to grow up. My husband John has written a book on the subject of these kinds of delays in development and a second one on the matter of reparenting as a treatment. There is no need for me to rehearse these ideas here.

Over time our students begin to mature and reflect on their lives both on campus and in what they customarily term "the real world." They take pride in the ranch community and recognize that there is always struggle to live together in a civil way. They ponder questions about the importance of rules and fairness, how to address the cruelty of bigotry, and think about how best to create a safe community for healing. These are eternal questions that have their echoes in ancient Greece or in any small-town meeting. They are as "real" here as anything in the world beyond the ranch.

My task at Montana Academy has been to sort through the many students who are referred to us and to select those whose troubles I feel we can best treat and who are likely to form a constructive community and to go on to live productive lives. On this front line I had daily contact with parents on the phone and in person. I witnessed their anguish over sending a beloved son or daughter away from home, and their despair at being so far away from them in a time of need. I have often worried that we did not do enough to connect them with the daily lives of their children and that they continued to suffer even when their son or daughter had made the adjustment to a new place and forged the relationships that gave them comfort and put smiles back on their faces.

I remembered my own parents' decision to send me off to boarding school in England in the early 1960s while they were living in the Middle East and how later when I graduated from Cambridge University and left for the US with my American husband they did their best to stay in touch from a distance. One of the ways they attempted to grasp my new life in a country that they did not know was to listen on the radio to the weekly broadcast of Alistair Cooke's "Letter from America." Cooke's first letter was written the year I was born, and he continued to write and read his letters on the radio for fifty years, providing a view of America that was both intimate in its detail and also broad in its dimension. It was the highlight of my parents' week.

I made the decision to take a similar tack and to write a monthly letter for parents of students at Montana Academy that would address both broad community issues and ideas as well as ground them in the natural world of northwestern Montana where we live and work with our students in a remote and lovely valley. Over the months and years these letters were sustained with the gratitude of parents who, in turn, sent me books and articles and told me that they had paid me the compliment of sending my letters on to family and friends.

There are now a considerable number of letters in my files and, with the help of my oldest daughter, Fiona, I have drawn on these to compile twenty-three letters and to arrange them, not in the order in which they were written, but rather in three parts. The letters in part I, "The Ranch," dwell on the physical location of Montana Academy, as well as on its roots in particular traditions and circumstances. Part 2, "The Community," contains letters that describe various aspects of this unusual therapeutic community, removed from the intrusion of modern social media, and the values that we attempt to inspire in our students in contrast to the problems of the communities in which they floundered and failed to grow up. The final letters in part 3, "The World Beyond," look beyond this ranch community to the wider world, into which our students return and where they will take up their young adult lives.

Candace Gaudiani, a dear friend whom I have known since I first arrived in America over forty years ago, has developed exceptional talent as a photographer to national acclaim and has collaborated with me to bring a visual dimension to these letters.

I want to dedicate this work not only to my husband John and partners John and Carol Santa who co-founded Montana Academy, but also to all the caring parents and wonderful young people who have enriched my work and life over the past fifteen years.

PART I

THE RANCH

1. LOST TRAIL RANCH

How many of you, I wonder, have driven down Lost Prairie Road, past the turnoff to the ranch and on down into aptly named Pleasant Valley? Now that spring has finally arrived in full force, I encourage you to take the time to enjoy a leisurely drive into the glorious back country of this corner of Montana.

Approximately four miles past the ranch's cattle guard on the left, you will find the Pleasant Valley rural school, one of the few remaining one-room schools in Montana. And a little further down the road you will arrive at a T-junction. Turn right and you will enter Lost Trail Ranch, an 8,000-acre wildlife preserve. You can continue on this road for the next 20 miles past Dahl Lake, and loop back along the shore of Bitterroot Lake to end up at the Hilltop Inn on Highway 2 in Marion. This adds a few miles to the usual trip back to town, but you will be rewarded for the effort.

In 1990 a Los Angeles developer bought Lost Trail Ranch and hired Jerry and Sherma Cundall from Wyoming to build a 900-head cow-calf operation on the last great working ranch in Northwest Montana. The ranch itself was the consolidation of at least two former homesteads in this lush valley, which had served as the staging ground for a near-forgotten railway line meant to connect Kalispell with Libby via Marion.

Montana Academy has a history with Lost Trail Ranch. At the end of our first summer of 1997 we needed a place to house girls off-campus, where they would be safe at night from the persistent attention of the boys. We met Sherma Cundall, a graceful mother of four grown children, who presided over the ranch from her large Victorian home. She agreed to take a group of girls under her care and to put them up in a small blue bungalow close to her house.

During the next two years while our girls lived on Lost Trail Ranch, the Cundalls began to spot wolves in the valley. In our first winter the pack was thought to consist of three adults and one pup, but by 1998 there was a large new litter. In 1999 Sherma recorded on video as many as ten wolves eating a roping calf, and the pack, now numbering around thirteen, was presenting a formidable threat to livestock in the valley. The Cundalls brought two Great Pyrenees dogs to protect the cattle, but they were no deterrent for the wolves. Sherma often took our girls with her in her truck when she did her nighttime rounds of the herd and carefully recorded on video and in her diary every wolf sighting. On February 13, 1999, she wrote that she sighted "six wolves, two of them dragging a newborn calf under the fence." By the end of 1999, 70 head of cattle were killed or missing. She recorded with bitterness that Defenders of Wildlife, which supposedly compensates ranchers, had only agreed that there was sufficient evidence to pay for three.

At the same time that wolves were preying on the cattle and calves of Lost Trail Ranch, Montana Power Company expressed an interest in saving Dahl Lake, a shallow algae-clogged pond at the eastern extreme of the ranch. They wished to use this wetland area as mediation for loss of wetland caused by the company's dam near Polson, at the southern end of Flathead Lake. The absentee owner of the ranch, who was having financial problems, accepted the company's offer of $5 million to dispose of it all. The US Fish and Wildlife Department took possession of the ranch, renaming it Lost Trail National Wildlife Refuge, and began to restore the floodplain to its historic role. This enhanced the survival prospects for various endangered and threatened species in the area: occasional grizzlies, lynx, eagles, and bull trout in the headwaters of the Fisher River.

Our girls moved back to campus and were housed in two trailers where the girls' dorm now stands. We built two cabins beside the dorm for the Cundall family, hoping to keep Sherma with the girls and Jerry to manage our ranch. In the end they stayed only a few months before, brokenhearted, they chose to move back to Wyoming.

Now Jack Cesaerone takes his summer field biology class to observe the behavior of red-winged and yellow-headed blackbirds in the marshes of Lost Trail Ranch, and our students currently bike there on weekends to prepare for upcoming challenge bike trips.

May and June are prime birding months in the Flathead Valley, and the Lost Prairie Road loop through Lost Trail Ranch to Marion is a particularly rewarding area for this pursuit. On a recent evening I was excited by a close sighting of a great gray owl sitting on a fence post beside the road, and by a stunning sea of blue camas lilies blooming close to the T-junction. The gray owl has been a campus regular, and last year I took all of the students out of study hall to view this gigantic bird sitting on a stump outside the ranch house.

We have ideal owl habitat, with large snags and plenty of open marshy ground for rodents. Thirteen of the 15 varieties of owls existing in the continental United States can be found here in Montana. Denver Holt, our local owl expert, has founded The Owl Institute in the Mission Valley and tracks snowy owls from their winter home here to their breeding grounds close to Barrow, Alaska. Some years ago I attended his weekend owl workshop and was rewarded not only by many sightings and the capture of a long-eared owl, but by the rapture of watching short-eared owls courting. In this spectacle, males fly to a considerable altitude to impress the females hidden below in the grass, and then drop suddenly while clapping their wings beneath their bodies.

This month I spotted many varieties of ducks—cinnamon and blue-winged teal, goldeneyes, buffleheads, ruddy ducks, and the gorgeously colored wood duck. A few weeks ago I was lucky enough to spot ten migrating avocets, resplendent with pink heads and black and white marked bodies, standing on a sandbar in the middle of a pond. All along Lost Prairie Road it is impossible to miss the meadowlarks sitting on the fence posts pouring out their melodious bursts of song and the frequent, brilliant flash of the western bluebird. If you visit us, perhaps you will also see the stately sand cranes picking their way though the marshlands. This is also raptor country. You are likely to see red-tailed hawks and chestnut-backed kestrels sitting along the electrical wires, and to spot the northern harrier flying low over the marshes. If you are really lucky you may spot golden eagles, as John did some years ago now on Lost Trail Ranch, where they often nest. John also spotted a bull moose in the pasture one morning last week.

As you cross the cattle guard into the ranch, you may notice a line of plastic tree preservers next to the stream, which is the headwaters of the Fisher River. Our Earth Clan[1] students planted several varieties of willows, cottonwoods and red osier dogwoods along the banks. We are in touch with the local agricultural agent who has promised to create a conservation and management plan for the ranch in the coming months.

Rick Stern has started his annual agricultural studies class focused on the science behind creating a fine vegetable garden. Adam Hannigan has almost finished his timber-frame greenhouse close to the barn, and this will lengthen the growing season for us next year. Each team is cleaning up the winter debris and weeding their particular flower beds. We look forward to holding team groups[2] outside in the summer sunshine, and to playing in the long evening light. We hope that you too will enjoy all of this when you visit.

---

1   Earth Clan is the beginning level for all students.

2   Team groups are held three times a week after lunch.

2. SPRING MIGRATIONS

APRIL 12, 2010

Meanwhile the wild geese, high in the clean blue air,
    are heading home again.
Whoever you are, no matter how lonely,
the world offers itself to your imagination,
calls to you like the wild geese,
    harsh and exciting—
over and over announcing your place
in the family of things.
                "Wild Geese" by Mary Oliver[3]

A couple of weeks ago we held our spring parent workshop. All of you came swooping in from your far-flung lives to Lost Prairie to join our students at Montana Academy. During these three days together we all experienced ourselves as part of a large and vibrant community. It never fails to give me great pleasure to watch parents sitting with their children in the lodge, and to join you in walking down the road as one long, strung-out, connected body.

Following the workshop, Dr. Cindy Grossman and I drove to the east side of the Rockies to view the annual migration of snow geese returning from their winter residence in the Central Valley of California to their breeding grounds in northern Canada. During the third week of March they reliably stop over at freezeout lakes, shallow man-made lakes of snowmelt runoff in the gently rolling short-grass prairie that grows in the rain shadow of the ragged, snowcapped, elongated "backbone of the world," as the Blackfeet called the front range of the Rockies.

When we arrived these lakes were dotted white with snow geese, sleeping and preening, calling to one another in rasping, gossipy cries after their long journey. Periodically some geese would lift off the lake to eddy and swirl in

---

3   Mary Oliver. "Wild Geese" from *Dream Work*. Boston: Atlantic Monthly Press, 1986.

the air currents, breaking away and rejoining the great flocks strung out across the blue skies. Toward dusk the entire lake, it seemed, ascended, lifting off in loose skeins of thousands and flew over our heads to land in the fields to glean the remains of last year's wheat and barley crops. We also rose to greet the assembled masses on the lake at dawn as they rose as a dense noisy swarm to feed again. It was an exhilarating sight, and one that humbles a person by its collective power. Birds bring beauty to our lives. We associate them with the times and settings in which we experience them. And we are fascinated by their migrations, courtships and songs. Millions of us have been entranced by the glorious film *Winged Migration*,[4] following the movements of various bird species, and by the extraordinary *March of the Penguins*,[5] a film about the Emperor Penguins caring for their eggs through the long Arctic winter. Birds also provide us with metaphors and images. My father used to refer playfully to my mother as "wuz," Arabic for goose, and when I was little he affectionately called me his "ugly duckling." I would have been hurt by this had I not also been taught that ugly ducklings grow up to be swans!

Some of our most moving poetry links us to the kingdom of birds and to our own consciousness. Wendell Berry's short poem, "To Know the Dark," is evocative:

> To go in the dark with a light is to know the light.
> To know the dark, go dark. Go without sight,
> and find that the dark, too, blooms and sings,
> and is traveled by dark feet and dark wings.[6]

Back at the ranch, David Long spent some time this winter working with his science students to train the ubiquitous campus ravens to come to the porch outside his classroom for food. Now David is turning his attention to

---

4   *Winged Migration*, directed by Jacques Cluzard, Michel Debats and Jacques Perrin. Culver City, CA: Sony Pictures Classics, 2003.

5   *March of the Penguins*, directed by Luc Jacquet, co-produced by Bonne Pioche and National Geographic Society, 2005.

6   Wendell Berry. "To Know the Dark" from *Farming: A Handbook*. NY: Harcourt Brace, 1970.

designing a morning-long field biology course for our summer block, which will look at aquatic ecosystems in and around the ranch, studying food webs, nutrient cycles, predator–prey relationships, human impact and biodiversity. The road into campus crosses the headwaters of the Fisher River, one of the many sources of the Columbia, and one that floods each spring. We have built up the road, but the river still flows abundantly and there are numerous vernal pools around the ranch that attract a wide variety of wild fowl to nest and provide a rich environment of insect and other aquatic life for exploration.

We encourage students to observe the natural world around them, just as we also train them to observe their inner worlds. One of our recent graduates has gone to study vervet monkeys for five months in South Africa and sends back copious emails detailing her experiences with both monkeys and humans. She writes: "One thing that I have noticed is that most of us come from some sort of troubled past. Though I am the only person here who has gone through some form of 'treatment,' scars on arms, addictions and fronts are easily seen on almost everyone.... At times I think that if we all had perfect self-esteem and normal histories this place would suck and the monkeys wouldn't get the love that they do get."

A *New York Times Magazine* article (January 31, 2010) on ecopsychology—a branch of psychology now taught as part of various college curricula—explores the impact on humans of living in closer harmony with nature or the lack thereof. This school of thought relies heavily on the ideas of Gregory Bateson, husband of Margaret Mead and a fellow anthropologist writing in the 1970s, who emphasized the interdependence of mind and nature. I can only report that my own life seems both richer and more peaceful when I am sensitive to the natural environment in which I live.

Many first-time visitors to our campus are moved by its beauty and remark that they can easily imagine that healing occurs in this lovely place. We feel lucky to do our clinical work in this setting and, when students get ready to leave, they note how busy and overwhelming the world outside Lost Prairie feels and express how much they will miss both the natural environment and community of the ranch. It is a pleasure to share it with you all. We hope that you, like the migrating birds, will be regular visitors.

3. COMMUNITY

DECEMBER 10, 2008

Every year Montana Public Radio holds a fundraising drive, just as NPR does in every state in the country. Although I am generally allergic to fund drives, this is one that I always enjoy. People from all over the state make gifts of appreciation in the form of donations: cheesecake, goats, fresh bantam eggs, raspberries in season, fly-fishing trips, respite for a caregiver, or a special weaving. The list is as great as the local talent and imagination. Every donation, no matter how small, receives public acknowledgment on the air, and I listen with my ear cocked in appreciation for the names of friends and neighbors both close at hand and far-flung across this large but sparsely populated state. The week ends with a grand finale "war" between those who donate on the part of their dogs and those who donate in the name of their cats.

Why do I enjoy this? I think it is because this is the one time of year when Montana seems like a village. We are all there listening with a common purpose. We all care and want to keep our NPR lifeline functioning, and we feel like one large interconnected family, despite the distances that separate us. We feel like a community.

We adults can assess how important a real community is in our lives. Moving from place to place is an inescapable fact of American life. Many of us have moved several times, and we know how difficult it is when we miss a network of support or find that our own social connections are spread too thin. Robert Putnam, the Harvard sociologist and author of *Bowling Alone*,[7] has posited a triangle with three points: 1) where you sleep; 2) where you work; and 3) where you shop. He suggests that the smaller the triangle the happier the human being, as long as there is social interaction to be had. He suggests that commuting is connected to social isolation, which causes unhappiness, and

---

7   Robert Putnam. *Bowling Alone: The Collapse and Revival of the American Community*. NY: Simon & Schuster, 2000.

notes that "every 10 minutes of commuting results in 10% fewer social connections." Certainly I have found myself happiest in those places where I encounter friends and neighbors on the street. I enjoyed this as an undergraduate in the relatively small market and university town of Cambridge, England, and again, more recently, in Kalispell. I know that I enjoy the annual NPR fundraiser because it serves to heighten my sense of community.

Our students crave this sense of belonging, although few of them are able to articulate this need. Many have felt isolated at home and have failed for various different reasons to develop a supportive and successful network. Some have simply sequestered themselves or joined an on-line virtual community to meet this basic human need. Others have fallen in with a group that accepts all comers and, while offering a bulwark against loneliness, provides little real support or caring.

Here on our isolated campus we have tightened Putnam's "triangle" to create a short walk from dorms to meals and lessons. Most students come to rely on the intimate sense of attachment and support that Montana Academy at its best provides. They feel recognized and known by adults and peers and are held accountable for delivering the best of themselves to others. Many of them tell us that this is what they miss most when they leave campus. They find that a sense of belonging is hard to recreate and takes time.

Skyhouse[8] students learn this lesson the hard way when they move into town and endure a certain amount of loneliness after the intimacy of ranch life. We deliberately subject them to this transition so they will begin to learn how to make new social connections without falling back into old and dysfunctional habits and how to build the skills to enter college life.

Parents also join the Montana Academy community. At the end of October you all took the time and trouble to make the long journey out to Lost Prairie for our three-day parent workshop. You attended lectures, contributed to groups, met with teachers and therapists, and spent time with your children in the lodge and around campus. We took a walk together out the driveway, across the cattle guard and down Lost Prairie Road.

---

8   Skyhouse is a transition program in Kalispell for older students who have completed a
     year or more on campus.

Twice each year we look forward to these occasions for you to come to campus en masse to join our staff and each other in this common task of helping to raise your children. Many of you tell me that you are touched to find yourselves meeting so many other fine people in the same difficult position of having to send a well-loved child far from home for help. You make new bonds, find support from other parents, and come away with a better sense of your child's life at Montana Academy.

I originally conceived of these monthly letters from Lost Prairie as a way to combat the isolation that parents feel when they must endure physical distance from their children, and to help you, too, to feel a part of their lives. Just as the yearly Montana Public Radio fund drive serves to make us Montanans feel a sense of connection across this large state, I hope to remind you that you are also a vital part of the extended Montana Academy community.

4. THE WORLD AROUND US

AUGUST 4, 2010

When I moved to Montana twenty years ago this month I was struck with what a friendly place it seemed to be. People passing by on back roads invariably raised a hand in greeting, and I rarely took a flight in or out of Kalispell without meeting someone I knew. Strangers on Main Street generally smiled at one another. Some of this small-town feeling has persisted over the years that I have spent here, and parents often share delightful stories about chance meetings with local people who mention Montana Academy favorably and reassuringly.

I have over the years attributed this friendliness to the fact that Montana is sparsely populated and that its people feel like they belong to an extended series of small towns spread over vast distances. They feel like neighbors who might at any moment require assistance from one another. Recently I have come to think that there is something else at work here.

My new understanding comes from reading *The Spirit Level*,[9] a book written by two British professors of Medicine and Epidemiology, Richard Wilkinson and Kate Pickett. The thesis of this book is that equality is better for everyone. The authors draw on a vast array of data collected by sources such as the US Census, UNICEF, and the WHO on the effects of excessive disparity of wealth and status. The book is filled with graphs that show the impact of great wealth inequality in various countries and by state on a vast range of matters that affect our lives: violence, imprisonment, drugs, life expectancy and health, but also obesity, educational performance, the position of women in society, social trust and mental disease—to name but a few. Everywhere we look, it seems, the measure of success is growth, and yet, as affluent societies have grown richer,

---

9   Richard Wilkinson and Kate Pickett. *The Spirit Level: Why Greater Equality makes Societies Stronger.* NY: Bloomsbury Press (US), 2010.

there have been long-term rises in rates of anxiety, depression and numerous other social problems.

The statistics Wilkinson and Pickett quote in chapter 3, "How Inequality Gets under the Skin," are alarming. There has been a profound rise in the anxiety level of the US population from 1953 to 1993. Among adolescents, this is accompanied by an increase in the frequency of behavioral problems, crime, alcohol and drug use. The authors speculate that, although there is a general long-term trend toward greater self-esteem, this is largely a fragile, defensive denial of weakness and manifests also as a rise in narcissism. By 2006, two-thirds of American college students scored above the average narcissism score in 1982. They suggest that both anxiety and narcissism have common roots in an increased concern about how one is perceived by others. They note that one of the most common triggers for violence is the feeling that one is looked down upon or disrespected.

Adolescents, in particular, experience enormous pressure from peers and worry endlessly about how they look and measure up. In the US, where inequality is greatest, six percent of children have been diagnosed with ADHD and almost ten percent of children aged three to seventeen had moderate or severe difficulties "in the areas of emotions, concentration, behavior, or being able to get along with other people." In Britain, another highly unequal society, the results are no better. As in the US, a much higher percentage of the population suffers from mental illness today than in recent past decades. The value that people in these more unequal cultures place on acquiring money and possessions creates a greater risk for depression, anxiety, substance abuse and personality disorder. I could go on and on, but suggest that some of you may wish to read The Spirit Level for yourselves.

One of the messages that I take away from this book is that trust cannot thrive in such an unequal world. The greater the degree of inequality, the less caring people are with one another and the less mutuality there is in relationships. Trust helps people feel secure and see others as cooperative and not competitive. The more we have, the more we need, and the more time we spend striving for material wealth at the expense of our family, relationships and quality of life. Montana ranks relatively high in the equality index, and the level of trust is also generally high. Therefore people tend to wave to each other in a friendly way on the back roads. John and I feel fortunate to have raised our three daughters here.

You may be wondering what all this has to do with your children, although of course you will have surmised the general drift of this argument. Perhaps many of you have already read Madeline Levine's book *The Price of Privilege* (2006).[10] Levine understands that there is a constant interaction between our own psychology and the pressures of the communities we live in. She closely examines the struggles of privileged families and, although her book was published before *The Spirit Level*, she well understands the problems that affluence can bring. She reports that affluence generally means that someone is working overtime, that high-powered husbands or wives can often be physically and emotionally unavailable, and that the homebound parent may become over-involved and intrusive with the kids. Expectations for high achievement and emphasis on external markers of success lead to perfectionism and depression. Levine asserts that the culture of affluence works against the development of the self, and she underlines the importance of encouraging children to develop internal motivation and to downplay the importance of external motivation. In the end we all want teenagers to feel effective in the world, to have a sense that they are in control of their lives, and to develop deep and enduring relationships with others, as well as to take care of themselves and know and accept who they are.

These goals are very much in line with those that we hope to achieve by the time our graduates are ready to leave Montana Academy. They are launching into a complicated world, one where they will experience the multiple noxious effects of inequality. My hope is that they will engage with the many energetic young adults who are joining forces to combat our profligate waste of the world's resources, and that their experience of a relatively harmonious and trusting small community here in Montana will have fortified their sense of themselves as separate from material possessions and will have given them the impetus to stand up and speak out, contributing to an important societal wake-up call.

---

10   Madeline Levine. *The Price of Privilege: How Parental Pressure and Material Advantage Are Creating a Generation of Disconnected and Unhappy Kids.* NY: Harper Collins, 2006.

5. OLD WINE IN NEW BOTTLES

JANUARY 14, 2009

n November, I accompanied John to the East Coast, where he gave lectures on the developmental model used at Montana Academy to students and faculty at Middlebury College and to psychiatrists at the Harvard Psychiatric Grand Rounds in the Beth Israel Hospital in Boston. At the end of this New England journey we spent a night with a family who had sent their son to Montana Academy when we first opened in 1997. This visit took place close to Concord, and we paused on our way back to Boston to think about the role of the Transcendentalists who moved westward in the 1840s away from what they perceived to be the distracting and aggressively commercial materialism of the Boston establishment.

This small group of like-minded people—among them Emerson, Thoreau, Alcott and Hawthorne—sought refuge in the countryside to pursue the solitude necessary for self-exploration, and drew upon threads of Classical and Romantic ideas to formulate their own notions about how to live their lives. Bronson Alcott, father of the more famous Louisa May, decided on a teaching career and was attracted to the ideas of the Swiss educator Johann Heinrich Pestalozzi (1746–1827) as a foundation for his own educational idealism: 1) Personality is sacred and inner dignity is to be respected in children as well as adults; 2) In each child is the promise of his or her potential; 3) Love of those we would educate is the sole and everlasting foundation in which to work. Alcott opened Temple School in Boston to pursue his vision of educating young minds, and this experiment became an inspiration to many educators. His ideas spread west and back to Great Britain, where schools were founded following Alcott and Pestalozzi's principles.

Henry David Thoreau (1817–1862) is arguably the best known and most accessible voice in this chorus. As a newly minted graduate of Harvard

College, he questioned the value of that experience and wondered what to do with his life. His documented personal journey while removed from society at Walden Pond is regularly taught in most American high schools and in Jason Rasco's English class at Montana Academy. Thoreau embarked on an inner journey that was an exercise "in living at one with the cosmos, in finding and dwelling within a unity that was physical, intellectual and spiritual."[11]

Thoreau names at the outset the core values that he aspires to: simplicity, independence, magnanimity, and trust. As the first steps in this process are simplicity and independence, I naturally find myself thinking that therein is an analogy to the common wilderness experience of our students, which often reaches its peak in a "solo."[12] Although our students do not undertake the self-imposed structure of the two years, two months and two days Thoreau allotted himself, they are nevertheless isolated from the distractions of society and asked to pursue an inner journey focused on self-examination, which they later continue in our remote location.

One of the pleasures of a long life is the ability to watch ideas wax and wane and reappear in new guises. I grew up with the poems of the English Romantics Wordsworth and Coleridge but had no idea of their influence in the New World. When John and I met 38 years ago at Cambridge University, he introduced me to the poems of Wallace Stevens, about whom he had written his Harvard English Literature thesis. We used one of these poems, "Final Soliloquy of the Interior Paramour," in our wedding service. Other poems too have stood the test of time and show a clear relationship to the Transcendentalist movement. "The Plain Sense of Things" even refers to a pond:

> ...The great pond,
> The plain sense of it, without reflections, leaves,
> Mud, water like dirty glass, expressing silence

---

11   Richard G. Geldard, ed. *The Essential Transcendentalists*. NY: Penguin Group, 2005, p. 95.

12   A "solo" is time spent alone and in contemplation in the wilderness for 24-48 hours.

Of a sort, silence of a rat come out to see,
The great pond and its waste of the lilies, all this
Had to be imagined as an inevitable knowledge.
Required, as a necessity requires.

Stevens, like Thoreau and Emerson, sought his own direct experience of life and trusted his own "plain sense of things." Montana Academy was founded on similar ideas—a willingness to trust our own experience and to use it to shape a new kind of hybrid school set apart in nature for psychological healing and self-exploration. While you all know that we have no particular spiritual affiliation and do not practice any form of worship, we do take seriously our role in shaping a moral education and in teaching our students to respect the natural world and to pay attention to their inner thoughts and experiences. We believe that the moral compass needs to exist inside each person and not necessarily between the covers of books. I have come to think that Montana Academy is, both in its location and its intent, a psychological heir to this nineteenth-century American movement.

6. THE STORIES WE TELL
ABOUT OURSELVES

JUNE 11, 2007

Not long ago, we had a visit from Joe Hannigan, faculty member of the Kellogg School of Business at Northwestern University and the parent of one of our weekend employees. He came to speak to our staff about the importance of the stories that organizations tell about themselves, or that others tell about them, and the ways in which these stories reflect the values of the organization and become part of the mythology shared by a community.

It is time to retell a story that we often relate when new families visit our campus and ask how we came to be here in this remote Montana valley. It is a story that the four of us share and we all tell it in our own ways, with common elements that we take from one another and our shared memories. It is the story of the founding of Montana Academy.

The idea for a therapeutic boarding school grew out of a number of diverse experiences. John and Carol Santa were themselves frantic parents of an adopted adolescent son who was bent on a course of failure in high school in the early '90s. They cast around for help locally and heard about the CEDU campus at Rocky Mountain Academy, just across the Idaho border. They placed their son there, attended parent workshops, and began to think about the benefits of such an approach, as well as ways that professional involvement, which the CEDU schools eschewed, could improve the process of family healing.

Meanwhile, John McKinnon had left a frustrating practice in adolescent in-patient psychiatry in Texas, where the encroachment of managed care on the relationship between psychiatrist and patient had curtailed treatment to fit the time allotted by insurance companies rather than the needs of the patients. Montana was a few years behind Texas in succumbing to the straightjacket of managed care, but soon after John had created an in-patient team at Pathways Treatment Center in Kalispell, he found his work undermined by the opposing tides of requests to fill beds and then empty them as quickly as possible. He could no longer tolerate a practice of medicine that undermined his fiduciary responsibility toward his patients. He and John Santa became friends while rallying the state's mental health practitioners and hospitals to provide an in-state solution to the Medicaid mental health crisis. When Montana, in its wisdom, chose to grant the contract to a large out-of-state organization, they gave up in disgust.

The four of us came together around the kitchen table in November 1996 to sketch the outline for a new approach to adolescent treatment that would provide steady, skillful psychotherapy and attentive family work, while not neglecting education. We wanted a relaxed setting, allowing time for therapy and development to unfold without intrusion from the outside world. By January we had a business plan, and by March John Santa's brother Scott, a real estate agent, had helped us locate the Lost Horizon Ranch down Lost Prairie Road off Highway 2. We took out second mortgages on our homes and got to work.

But there was one glaring hole in our plans. We had no idea how we would connect with the students and families we hoped to serve. We were operating on a Field of Dreams fantasy: Build it and they will come!

Sometime in early 1997 John McKinnon spent a weekend with his father in Marin County and spoke with an old friend about his plans for a special school. She wondered if he had heard of educational consultants. When he inquired as to what such a professional did, she gave him the name of Virginia Reiss. When they met over coffee, John described our plans. Ginny told him that if we were to succeed in this venture, we would be unique in the country. She offered to help by introducing us to her fellow professionals. A few weeks later, two groups of these consultants flew in from around the country to meet with us. As we listened to their questions our task became clearer, and this dialogue began to inform our vision. They began to refer us students. And since we were brand new and eager for any new referral, we had no idea which kinds of problems we were ready to handle, and we did not know that it might sometimes be important to turn students away.

We opened the campus in the third week of June 1997 for an eight-week summer program, expecting that we might serve eight to ten students at most. Instead we opened our doors with twenty-one students! They arrived over a period of five days, toting sacks of belongings and looking with contempt upon the shabby ranch house and the unfinished boys' dorm. We still look back on that first summer as one of the most stressful periods of our lives, rivaled only by becoming parents for the first time. At the end of those early long days on campus, we would finally arrive home exhausted, but rarely able to sleep. We all lay awake staring at the ceiling, wondering whether the campus and its residents would still be there upon our return in the morning.

Sometimes it was touch and go indeed. Some students feasted on mushrooms found on a camping trip. Others held blanket parties at night. One found unlocked gasoline to huff and brought cigarettes into the dorm. Daily they demonstrated all the possible ways to create potential catastrophes. We followed behind, securing the latest loopholes, trying to create structure and to provide the foundation for a community, building relationships one student at a time. Phil Jones brought order in the classroom—a small island of sanity in the swirling melee. As I remember, the students were reading *The Lord of the Flies* that summer, and this became our metaphor for the peril of a community in which adults were not adequately in control and students were potentially dangerous. John Santa led hikes in Glacier Park. Our young staff worked tirelessly at every task imaginable. John McKinnon hospitalized out-of-control students at our local psychiatric facility until their parents could come to read them the riot act and get them moving in the right direction. At the end of the summer four students left and the remaining seventeen stayed on (fifteen boys and two girls) to form the first Montana Academy graduating class of 1998.

So what does this founding story tell us? Certainly in our memories it lives on as a story of a vision, of persistence despite the threat of anarchy and the terrible fear of failure. It tells us of the need for systems and order, of lessons learned during the task of forming a community both of students and of staff, of the bonds that relationships can bring. It tells us of the extraordinary trust and determination of parents in the face of adversity.

Today's orderly community is a far cry from the chaos of ten years ago, and we take special pride in the vibrancy and warmth of relationships between our staff and students. We still depend, as we always will, on the support of parents, and we thank you for your partnership in shaping this healthy environment.

PART II

THE COMMUNITY

You are a wonderful
Person. your Parents
Sent you here so you
Could Become even Better
and get help with the hard
stuff your Parents Love you
Very much. If they Didn't
They wouldn't have Done
anything
Be Happy I ♥ U

7. SENDING A CHILD AWAY

JUNE 10, 2010

When parents come to interview at Montana Academy on behalf of their son or daughter, they often express their grief about having to send a beloved child far from home to grow up with strangers. Many parents tell us that one of the hardest things that they have ever done is to call transporters to remove an unruly child from her bedroom at four o'clock a.m. to take her to a wilderness program. At the time of enrollment on our campus students have generally had an initial stab at reconciliation with their parents during their course of wilderness treatment and have themselves more or less accepted the necessity of leaving home to finish their high school education. They generally say that they are nervous about entering a new school, but they rarely shed tears. Parents almost invariably do.

The months, and even years, preceding an enrollment have often been an extraordinarily wretched time in parents' family life, precipitating serious marital stress on top of the misery of watching a loved child endanger his future or sometimes her life. Yet many parents continue to experience intense loss for several months after enrollment. They are acutely aware of the empty bedroom and the hole in their hearts. One mother told me that she avoided going to the grocery store at times when she might run into someone she knew and have to endure questions about her child that she could hardly bear to answer. This grief is mixed with the concomitant shame of feeling like a defective parent. Sadness over a child's premature departure from home is surely easy for any of us to understand, and yet I come from a culture in which parents were made of sterner stuff.

The British public school has been around for several hundred years. Some accounts of life at such schools were not pleasant. Students were routinely toughened up by regular floggings and cold showers. Masters were often cruel, and "fagging"—a system of servitude by new boys as the vassals of older boys or prefects—was the norm. Sexual acting out was also routine, if not actively condoned. Britain's oldest public school, Rugby, was founded in 1567 and, with the publication of Tom Brown's *School Days* in 1857, became a model for a first-rate Victorian education. Charlotte Bronte published *Jane Eyre* ten years earlier in 1847, giving an account of young Jane's excruciating experience of hunger, cold and punitive instruction at Lowood School. Yet British parents who could afford to do so sent their children away to boarding schools in the hope of instilling certain kinds of values and providing an education that was not available at home.

My parents were living in the Persian Gulf when my brother Peter turned seven, and I remember returning to England with my mother to accompany my little brother, who was still sucking his thumb and stroking his "blankie," to his enrollment at a prep school in Oxford. This school was the first step on the road to Oxbridge. Although I was two years his senior, because I was a girl I remained with my parents until I was twelve years old, and only then was likewise enrolled at a girls' boarding school in Wiltshire for the next five years of my life.

Neither my brother nor I found this an easy adjustment but we, and our parents, accepted it as the natural order of things and a necessary part of growing up. This was simply a routine part of upper-middle-class British culture. My tenderhearted mother grieved a great deal but she kept it to herself. I don't ever recall a complaint while she got on with the job of being a diplomat's wife in the Middle East and doing her best to help others less fortunate than her own children. We communicated by weekly letters exchanged across great physical and temporal distances as we got on with the business of growing up. English literature of the time is replete with stories of children separated from their parents by the month-long sea voyage to India. *Little Black Sambo*, written by one such Scottish mother for the young children that she had left in England before returning to India, was one of my earliest books.

I am inclined to think that American parents are not suffering any more or less than their British counterparts of an earlier generation in sending their sons and daughters away to school. I think that it is rather a matter of cultural expectations. My father, an only child who had lost his father at age two, was raised by a doting mother. His maiden aunts considered him spoilt, in danger of "not learning to tie his own shoes," and packed him off to a local Oxfordshire boarding school at age ten. He always told me that he was terribly unhappy there but that he learned what it took to be successful and worked hard for a place at Oxford University. My mother, who was one of six children whose father died when she was 13, helped to raise her younger siblings and earned a scholarship to nearby Queen's University, Belfast. My parents were grateful for their hard-earned educations and were determined to do whatever it took to ensure that their own two children also received good educations. They saved their money carefully and were thankful that they could afford to do this duty. This was by no means unusual.

I also believe that, since Montana Academy opened its doors in 1997, there has been a significant cultural change in acceptance of the necessity of sending some young people away from home to therapeutic boarding schools or other programs. Now I often hear that visiting parents have met or talked with someone else who has either sent a student to us or to some other place-ment. Parents are increasingly willing to talk to and support each other in making these hard decisions. Many educational consultants are now offering support groups as part of their outreach to parents who seek their advice and expertise. Parents are no longer so alone, and this makes the sense of shame and loss more bearable. One mother wrote to me recently to tell me that her sister-in-law was worried about her college-age daughter and had expressed her envy that her nephew had dealt with his difficulties when he was a teenager and that it was possible to maintain a sense of normalcy (school, exercise, friends, chores and trips with clear boundaries and tight structure) sooner rather than later. We all hear stories of young adults whose lives remain in jeopardy because their parents couldn't, or wouldn't, make the necessary commitment whether they liked it or not. And there is considerable press currently about "basement boys," young men (and women) still living in their parents' homes long after they should be out on their own. Current statistics suggest that 64 percent of college graduates are back in the nest. A recent *New Yorker* cover (May 24, 2010) depicts one such young man moving back into his room where he hangs his PhD certificate on the wall, while his anguished parents watch from the doorway. While this reflects the changing economic climate, it may also be indicative of a broad cultural failure to help children grow up.

Some of our students manage to spontaneously express their gratitude to their parents for having made the hard decision to send them away and for investing in their futures. One young man about to leave campus in May wrote to his parents, "I guess that I have never really thanked you guys for sending me here. When I am struggling or even when things are going well, I forget how much you guys sacrifice to help me.... I know that you would do it over again without hesitation.... I want to make you proud more than anything else and to show you how much the last year and a half has meant to me." What parent would not be overjoyed to receive such a letter?

Our students sometimes joke about sending their own kids away from home to wilderness when they reach those difficult teenage years, and although I certainly hope that this is not necessary, I am amused by the sentiment. Transporters[13] and wilderness treatment have become a singular rite of passage for a small group of privileged youth who toss around the supposed virtues and restrictions of ending up in one or other therapeutic placement. While this new culture does not yet hold the status of the most famous English public schools of Eton and Winchester, it also amuses me to think of parents and students assessing the relative merits of Carlbrook versus Montana Academy!

---

13   Transporters are people whom parents hire to take their reluctant children safely to treatment.

8. WHAT IS "THERAPY" ANYWAY?

FEBRUARY 23, 2009

Periodically I join a group, or run one when a therapist is absent. This is an opportunity for me to dip into the ongoing clinical work at Montana Academy and test the waters to see what our students are learning. Recently I sat in on a group with a boys' team. They spent the first half hour talking about their concerns and anxieties in preparation for the addition of a new student who was arriving that afternoon. They were thoughtful, remembering their own arrivals with their attendant confusion and sense of being overwhelmed. They also valued the gains that they had made, the comfort that they took in their team, which had not had a new member in some months, and their worry that a new student would upset the cohesion of the existing group. Yet they were at pains to tell each other that it was important to set the tone of the team so that the new student would find them functioning well and discover a culture where he would be expected to do the same.

We turned to the subject of therapy and I asked them what they thought "therapy" actually was. One student said that he really didn't know, but that he was struggling just to be honest about what he was thinking and feeling. He said that his father didn't think much of therapy but that his mother "believed it was helpful." This was confusing as he began to have a better relationship with his father and cared what he thought. Another said that he saw his mother using therapy for advice and he was skeptical about this approach.

One young man said that he thought he was doing therapy all day long, not just with his therapist in the office, but with his friends in serious conversations and with staff he had come to know. He was trying to increase his self-awareness, to say what was on his mind and to work on improving his relationships, knowing that Montana Academy would help him avoid "crashing and burning" as he had done at home.

A fourth, who had been at Montana Academy for 18 months, said he didn't really think about being in therapy anymore, but his therapist and team leader were so much a part of his everyday life that consideration of their thoughts and approach was integrated into everything he did. Not one young man referred to therapy as something that was done to him or as a set of learned skills. Each one was, in his own unique way, attempting to follow a path of mindfulness and improvement of day-to-day relationships.

Some months ago John Santa urged me to see the film *Lars and the Real Girl*,[14] in which a depressed, lonely and help-rejecting young man, Lars, has a mail-order blow-up doll that he insists on treating as though it were a real girl-friend. At first his relatives and larger community are shocked and confused about how to treat this fantasy relationship, but gradually they decide to suspend normal expectations for his social behavior and settle into an accep-tance that this strange relationship must be important to him somehow and should not be denied.

The entire community behaves in an unusual manner. They go along with the fantasy. A compassionate physician deftly uses this imaginary relationship to treat the young man. When Lars is ready, he gradually lets go of his blow-up girlfriend and reenters the world of real relationships. Odd as this may sound, this is as moving and compassionate a depiction of therapy as I have ever seen. The community suspends judgment of strange behavior, loves and cares for Lars as he finds his way back to them.

Oftentimes our students need this same forbearance and understanding. One young woman developed a relationship with a plastic horse that she named and took everywhere with her, pretending to be its mother. She fed it, loved it and protected it from all teasing and flippant hurtful banter. She took this parenting role very seriously and resisted all suggestion from our well-meaning staff that she grow up and get over it. It turned out that this girl's parents had recently had a serious fight that had left her feeling scared and lonely. She sought refuge in her active fantasy life and acted it out, much as a younger child

---

14   *Lars and the Real Girl*, by Nancy Oliver, directed by Craig Gillespie, distributed by MGM studios, Beverly Hills, CA, 2007.

might do. Many of our other students tell outrageous lies and stories that serve to both hide and reveal their worries. While we regularly challenge students to move on from childish conduct, we also try to do this in the context of understanding what their behavior means and why they cling to it. We do our best not just to pay attention to the melody line of their chatter and actions, but also to listen for the sounds of deeper chords. There is, after all, an underlying meaning to most of human behavior and it is this meaning that we seek to understand in therapy, so we can be in tune with our young people in more than a superficial manner.

Thoughtful therapy is not something that can be imparted from books or seminars alone and it is much more than a set of skills that are delivered willy-nilly according to the adolescent's diagnosis. We are not simply in the business of instruction. It takes years to develop a "third ear," to hear the underlying themes of people's life stories and to help them learn to pay attention to their own thoughts, so that eventually they can do this for themselves. The physician in *Lars and the Real Girl* is such a skilled therapist, one who listens, understands, and does not simply confront or instruct, but patiently helps Lars ease his pain and move on in his life. Being heard and understood are the first steps in healing.

This therapeutic task of recognition is different from another aspect of work at Montana Academy: the push to grow up. We make this push explicit to our students. We challenge them to think not just about themselves, but about each other and the needs of their team or the larger community, and encourage them to distinguish between their own wishes and requirements and those of others. Adults recognize that these students have little empathy for others, and that values are rarely instilled by lectures or coercion. Instead we attempt to create some discomfort with their childish narcissism. Students are invited to express themselves honestly and clearly, but also to consider themselves in the context of relationships with teammates, staff and parents. We do not try to rescue them from the struggles of their own ambivalence about such tensions, and are glad to watch them wrestle with their own selfish wishes, knowing that if they indulge these they may hurt those who love and care for them. This is the work of growing up.

We also do our best to create the kind of community exemplified in *Lars and the Real Girl*—one in which individuals can be heard and feel deeply understood and where idiosyncratic behavior may be tolerated while a young person works through pain and misunderstanding to find his or her way back to solid real relationships with peers, staff and parents. Such is the healing offered in our therapeutic milieu.

We look forward to your joining us at the March parent workshop, where your physical presence completes the circle of this community.

9. SILENCE

This is the time of year when a great stillness settles into Montana. The skies are leaden, the snowflakes fall, and one's eye accustoms itself to the nuances of a grey palate. A few solitary ravens and small flocks of pied magpies fly across the white fields and pierce these quiet dark woods with their cries. The contrast inside the warm, bright lodge is dramatic. Green wreaths and boughs of fresh evergreens decorate the walls and stairwell and the community is animated by the excitement of another graduation with its attendant aura of elation and sweet sad partings.

I, for one, have come to have a deep appreciation for the benefits of silence. Here at Montana Academy we unplug your children from the world of mass communication and networking that governs the lives of most teenagers and many adults today. Off campus we have grown accustomed to the constant flow of noise as entertainment and information wash over us, and we are rarely separated for long from those instruments that connect us to each other and to the market forces that shape our lives. This always strikes me most powerfully when I leave Kalispell and enter the airways, where I am assaulted by continuous television broadcasting from all corners, punctuated by announcements and jabbering into cell phones. Most of us live in a society polluted by noise where we accustom ourselves to the background din just as we would do if we had to live and sleep next to a busy road. And yet I believe that it is hard to hear ourselves think in such an environment.

It takes time to accustom oneself to silence. One parent expressed her amazement, noting that she became nervous and fretful without the usual accompaniment of sound. It takes time for our students, too, to settle into the silence of this unplugged world. They naturally miss their social and musical connections. But when they do allow themselves to be still and quiet, the process of healing begins. They stop struggling so hard to get back to the known world and begin to listen to the still, small voice within themselves that expresses their own thought processes.

Skilled therapy respects this voice and helps cultivate it. Our students slowly learn to know how they really feel, to articulate it and search for its roots and branches in their lives. They begin to drop pretense and artificiality, say what they mean and mean what they say. They learn to listen for the note of authenticity in themselves and in others. They start to have real conversations, first with their teammates and then with the rest of the community. At first their interactions must be mediated by adults, as so often the electronic world has not been. Such conversations must be protected, supported and nurtured before they can be trusted to stand alone, but as the students and community mature the voices become strong and clear and the robust murmur of social time in the lodge reverberates with warmth against a background of music from guitars or piano. The community throbs with vitality and purpose. It has a life that is in stark contrast to the quiet stillness of winter outside and yet it is born of it. Such life, as always, arises from simple beginnings.

Small wonder then that the movie *Into Great Silence*,[15] filmed at the Grande Chartreuse, France's great Carthusian abbey in the Alps, has been a hit this year in New York City, where lines were long and the two-week showing in April was extended indefinitely. I believe we are all hungry for such silence and this may be one of the reasons that meditation practice has become so popular in recent years. We need the ability to hear our own thoughts, to manage our emotions and anxieties, and to be part of a community in which we can both listen, be heard ourselves, or be silent if we wish. Welcome to this community.

---

15 *Into Great Silence*, directed by Philip Gröning. NY: Zeitgeist Films, 2005.

10. MENTORSHIP

NOVEMBER 19, 2007

A few weeks ago I visited my ninety-year-old mother in a village just out-side Cambridge. I timed my visit to coincide with an alumni weekend at Cambridge University, an opportunity to revisit my alma mater and to attend an excellent variety of lectures laid on for the occasion. My favorite talk was conducted within the confines of the Plant Science Laboratory, which houses the Cambridge Herbarium. Lest you wonder, as I did, exactly what a Herbarium is, let me explain. The tall stacked cupboards in the narrow room contain fifty thousand dried plant specimens dating back some three hundred years. They house one of the world's great collections, which pro-vide the basis for naming living organisms and serves as a resource to which researchers from around the world turn for its unique record of the world's diversity and for its timeline of plant evolution.

Our speaker, Roger Parker, professor of Botany and Director of the Cambridge Botanical Gardens, spoke passionately about one predecessor, John Stevens Henslow (1796–1861). You are unlikely to have heard of him, but you all know the name of one of Henslow's students. Henslow himself was a polymath, a professor of metallurgy and a mathematician who then moved on to the Chair of Botany at Cambridge, which he occupied for twenty-five years before retiring as a clergyman. He was a prodigious scientist, who founded the Cambridge Botanical Gardens as a living laboratory in which to work out the relationship of varieties to species in the mutations that affect plant develop-ment and form. He was trying to understand the role of hybridization in nature.

In his day Henslow was famous for his Sunday country walks in and around Cambridge. He was regularly accompanied by a young undergraduate whose name was Charles Darwin. Darwin was known only for his beetle collection and his love of good food until he also became known as "the man who walks

45

with Henslow." For this loyalty Henslow recommended Darwin for the voyage of the good ship Beagle. In short, during that talk in the Herbarium I was looking at the very specimens Darwin collected on the Galapagos Islands. These, together with his observations on finches, became the basis for his thoughts on the evolution of the species!

⁓

Why do I bother telling you this story? Certainly I, who spent a good part of an English childhood pressing wild flowers, was excited to see this extraordinary collection. But in this story I also saw an example of the importance of mentorship.

My most memorable mentor was a small, unassuming Austrian woman whose name was Emma Plank, but whose friends called her Nuschi. At the age of 16 Nuschi left her home to work in the kitchen of a new experimental preschool, established in the post-WWI slums of Vienna. She studied Italian in the evenings in order to read and learn from the school's founder, Maria Montessori. She joined a select group of nursery school teachers interested in child development, which was run by Anna Freud, who was herself a preschool teacher. During this period a Danish student, traveling with a friend, arrived in Vienna looking for work. Anna Freud recommended this young man work with Nuschi at the Montessori preschool. And so she helped to train Erik Erikson, who became a Montessori pedagogue.

When Austria was invaded by Nazi Germany in 1938 Nuschi's young attorney husband, Robert Plank, was arrested briefly by the Gestapo. Soon after this they fled Vienna, along with many others of the Jewish intelligentsia. In London Nuschi and Robert ran a home for Basque refugee children. Later they immigrated to San Francisco, where they were welcomed by Erik and Joan Erikson. Nuschi established the first Montessori school in Pacific Heights, attended by many children of the city's psychiatrists and psychoanalysts.

Some years later Nuschi received an invitation to move to Cleveland, where a group of psychoanalysts had established a lay analytic training center. There she helped found the Hannah Perkins Nursery School, where psychoanalysts trained and taught. Years later, when I was a young social work student, I was lucky to receive my first training there, and to train also for a few months at the Anna Freud Hampstead Clinic. Nuschi was no longer working at the nursery school. She had moved to the west side of Cleveland where she had started the first Child Life Program to care for children hospitalized at Cleveland Metropolitan General Hospital. I acquired a small grant to work with her there in the summer of 1972. Each morning I drove to work with her from the east side of Cleveland and so learned the innovative ideas she had developed to prepare children for surgery and to help them live and play during extended periods in the hospital for broken bones, burns or cancers. She was gentle with both the children and her young staff, but firm in her convictions, which were solidly grounded in her practical training as a Montessori teacher and in a psychoanalytic theory of child development.

During our commute to and from work, Nuschi and I became friends. John, who was then a medical student, often joined me to dine with Nuschi and her courtly husband, who himself continued an intellectual life, writing literary essays about George Orwell in particular. This friendship survived our move to New Haven, where Nuschi helped me to secure a fellowship in child development and treatment at the Yale Child Study Center. After our next move to San Francisco, she and Robert introduced us to a wide circle of their Viennese friends. Some years later when Robert died in Cleveland, Nuschi returned to Vienna where she had a brother, two nieces and a handful of students who had kept in touch with her over the years. I did not see her again. I learned of her death in 1991, around the time we moved to Montana.

Mentorship at Montana Academy works at many different levels. New students are assigned to a student mentor whose job it is to help them through the first difficult days and weeks of adjustment. Many mentors work hard to do this job well, remembering their own struggles and taking pride in the progress and success of their mentees. Frequently the mentors are the ones to publicly announce a mentee's clan promotion to the community.[16]

Parents sometimes request their own parent mentor. I am always happy to help you make contact with an experienced parent who might be of help to

---

16   Students progress through five clans or levels during the program. They make a formal application for promotion to their treatment team.

a new one. In our clinical work with students, senior staff members mentor more junior ones. Therapists receive weekly supervision with one of the senior clinicians. All of us are open for consultation at any time and often develop close, lasting friendships. And so in this way we pass on our training and ideas to the next generation. I now understand Nuschi's generosity with me and Henslow's pleasure in his walks around Cambridge with his student whose fame would soon eclipse his own. There is no greater compliment than that a student should build on our foundation.

Nuschi's birthday was November 11. I still think of her and am grateful for her influence on my life. I like to think that she would have approved of Montana Academy. No doubt she would recognize in Lost Prairie strong evidence of her lasting influence.

11. SPRING DIGGING

MAY 7, 2009

have been a gardener most of my life. My interest in gardens is part of my English heritage and upbringing. My father was one in a long line of Cotswold farmers, and I spent several childhood holidays visiting cousins on their two-thousand-acre farm, where my aunts (one widowed and one never married) managed a small diverse holding with wheat and barley, sheep, pigs, chickens and horses. My job as a young child was to collect and wash the hens' eggs. My aunt Nancibel was president of the Oxford Farmers' Union and, as such, dressed in breeches with a tweed jacket and tie, delivered weekly farming lectures broadcast on the BBC. My father left Oxford for Jerusalem and a lifetime's work as a diplomat in the Middle East, but always returned to his roots deep in the Oxfordshire countryside and would take me walking among the fields and hedgerows of the Glyn Valley and to visit the elegant walled gardens of the Oxford colleges. When he retired and took up a new role as vicar of a small country parish in Leicestershire he kept an enormous vegetable and flower garden along with several hives of bees.

Family legend has it that early on I was a stickler for proper plant names: "Grandma, that's a banksia rose." At age twelve, I was accepted at St. Mary's Calne, my boarding school in Wiltshire, because during the interview with the headmistress I was thrilled to see sweet peas and wanted to pick them. She approved. Indeed we had school allotments that we tended eagerly in our spare time and my best friend and I competed on walks along the Downs for who could see and name the most flowers first. I was brought up discussing plants at the dinner table and my family now would tell you that I am capable of being a pedant on this subject.

By and large I have learned to keep this long-lived passion to myself except when I am around other enthusiasts. When I was in England last May my old school friend and I shared a glorious couple of hours wandering round the Cambridge botanical gardens, testing to see if we could still compete in our knowledge of flower names and teaching each other new ones! I never fail to visit some of my favorite college gardens there and was proud to have my college, New Hall, win a garden exhibit prize at the 2007 Chelsea Flower Show.

What does all this have to do with Montana Academy? In this first decade of MA's existence all of our energy has gone into producing an effective, first-rate therapeutic and academic program. There has been little time and attention for anything else. We are lucky to enjoy a stunning natural environment that, like some of Britain's country estates, requires relatively little embellishment. And yet, in the last couple of years we have been wondering if we are using this environment to its fullest potential.

You are all aware, I am certain, that there is a new movement afoot in the land to return to a more sustainable way of living and feeding ourselves locally. Who among us has not read Michael Pollan's *The Omnivore's Dilemma*,[17] which makes the case against large-scale and corporate agriculture? We have a small but strong local farmers' market that operates on Tuesday evenings in Whitefish and on Saturday mornings in Kalispell. Some of our Skyhouse students have enjoyed volunteering at various local farms in the summer and our upper-level campus students have loved weekend visits to the Purple Frog Gardens in Whitefish, where they have assisted in various gardening tasks in exchange for the pleasure of a simple local meal or a fun time in the dirt on a sunny day.

Our social studies teacher, Rick Stern, came to us from Missoula where he was involved in creating community gardens. He started a spring course in agricultural studies for our students. He took over a small organic garden beside the boys' dorm and experimented with the crops that might grow well in our exceptionally short summer growing season. Our long-time weekend staff Adam Hannigan spent much of last year working diligently with students to log and cut wood to build a timber-frame greenhouse so we could increase our growing season by sheltering some of the more tender vegetables. Last year we decided to move the major venue for our garden plot to the area beside the

17 Michael Pollan. *The Omnivore's Dilemma: A Natural History of Four Meals*. New York: Penguin Press, 2006.

arena. The greenhouse is already established there and we have put in a watering system. This year we will be tilling and fertilizing, creating a new and expanded vegetable garden under Rick's supervision.

All of this involves a significant commitment of manpower and working hours. Rick generally takes a six-week summer break and the garden has, in his absence, not been a serious priority. This year we will try to change this. We have hired an agricultural intern to run our campus flower and vegetable gardens with the students' help. We are expecting that all our students will participate at least minimally in this effort, working alongside our intern, and that those students who have more flexible schedules or a greater degree of interest will be working hard outdoors all summer long, especially on the weekends, to produce some of the food that will be enjoyed by our community.

What are our students likely to learn from this experience? I hope they will learn the work and patience necessary to grow anything worthwhile. I hope they will learn respect for the effort involved in putting food on the table and the satisfaction of hard work. Perhaps they will even find this an outlet for their frustrations. Along with weeding, I grew up with the Kipling story about "How the Camel got his Hump" and the poem that accompanies it with the following lines living on in my childhood memory:

> The cure for this ill is not to sit still,
> Or frowst with a book by the fire;
> But to take a large hoe and shovel also,
> And dig till you gently perspire.[18]

This has, in fact, proved to be a good outlet over the years, although John would, and does in his book, attest to another option offered by Seamus Heaney (who grew up on a farm in the same small Northern Ireland town as my mother) in his poem "Digging":

> Between my finger and my thumb
> The squat pen rests.
> I'll dig with it. [19]

---

18   Rudyard Kipling. *Just So Stories for Little Children.* New York: MacMillan, 1951.

19   Seamus Heaney. *Selected Poems 1966–1987.* New York: Noonday Press, Farrar, Strauss & Giroux, 1990.

Perhaps as students sow and dig they may also begin to attune their minds to the visible rather than the virtual and rediscover the natural world.

This vision of work and study in nature has very old roots going back to classical times. I have recently read *Gardens: An Essay on the Human Condition*[20] by Robert Pogue Harrison (2008) and was particularly struck by "Academos" in which he writes of the natural affinity between education and gardens. He discusses the founding of Plato's academy, located just outside the walls of Athens, which was a self-enclosed *paradeisos* for the privileged few, detached from the tumult of city life—a nursery for future statesmen. Socrates talked of sowing the seeds of truth using the analogy of soil and soul—both of which lend themselves to cultivation. Both the teacher and the gardener sow valuable seeds and nurture their growth to maturity. In Plato's secluded academy emphasis was placed on community, conversation and the fellowship of philosophy (therapy?), as well as on the love between teachers and their students. These too are the seeds that we hope to nurture in our gardens and in our students.

Spring has finally arrived in Montana and we hope that you will enjoy this with us when you visit.

---

20   Robert Pogue Harrison. *Gardens: An Essay on the Human Condition*. Chicago: University of Chicago Press, 2008.

12. VIRTUAL LIFE

MARCH 11, 2010

A couple of years ago I read a bizarre story in the *London Review of Books* (August 14, 2008) that has stuck with me. Jonathan Raban, an Englishman living and writing for some years now in the United States, wrote about the "Virtual life of Neil Entwhistle." Entwhistle emerged as a public figure in January 2006. He was at that time a twenty-seven-year-old educated at York University where he earned a degree in electronic engineering and met a young American woman, Rachel, whom he married and with whom he eventually moved to the States, where he attempted to earn a living as a digital entrepreneur. The couple had a baby and lived in the US for barely four months, posting frequent internet updates of the happy family, until Neil shot his wife and baby at point-blank range with a Colt .22 revolver that he had borrowed from his father-in-law's collection (driving forty-five minutes to collect the weapon and then to return it again after the shooting). Neil then boarded a plane for England where he was arrested. In his pockets were a one-page eulogy to Rachel, a draft of a scripted phone call to the editors of London tabloids regarding his side of the story, and an advertisement for the services of prostitutes and escort agencies.

Raban argues that there is no persuasive evidence for a motive in this murder and suggests strongly that a close examination of Neil's virtual history and the contents of his pockets at the time of his arrest "were like his on-line life, as he switched from screen persona to screen persona, switching identities and avatars on his internet journeys." Raban suggests that in the end Entwhistle lived his life in virtual space and that, although outwardly conforming and conventional, he "conspicuously lacked an authentic self."

What does this strange and extreme story have to teach us about the inner lives of those young people who are referred to us for help concerning their addiction to computers and video games, and who treat their lives on-line with more seriousness than their flesh-and-blood relationships? We are all familiar with the parental lament. A son or daughter has retreated into the on-line world, has begun to inhabit the twilight zone of the screen, has turned nights into days and become hooked on the computer as a source of emotional sustenance. We are also aware of how cruel others can be to needy young people. For some shy and awkward teenagers the internet has been a source of comfort, but at the same time it has deprived them of the necessity of venturing outside their comfort zone to make real relationships. Many of our students have become hypertrophied creatures of the night, masters of intricate war games and ersatz relationships. MySpace does not show the person as she really is, but in the various guises in which she chooses to present herself.

Neil Entwhistle lost himself in these guises. He did not know who he was, had little sense of reality in his life, and probably wanted to escape when that life failed to measure up to his fantasies of what it should be. He appears to have committed a murder without the slightest idea of what the obvious consequence was likely to be—just as one gets rid of an evil avatar in a game. Some of our teenagers, like younger children, are also at risk of mistaking fantasy for reality.

Modern technology has confused this normal developmental step of discerning reality by providing even very young children with a virtual existence that is distinctly separate from those of the adults in their lives. Cell phones have morphed into mini hand-held computers, social networking devices, cameras and tiny movie screens. Some teenagers use them to stay connected with the most important people in their lives, others to go underground and elude the watchful eyes of adults. Some get lost in an underworld of pretend. The outward trappings of connectivity are not always what they appear to be: they can readily aid and abet the secret lives of teenagers. Adults' attempts to regain control of their children's technological tools can provoke rage and sometimes violence.

One of our students recently told me that he was dismayed to think that his whole generation was awash in a world of drugs, pornography and on-line media, and that underneath all this they were struggling with enormous anxiety about how to find themselves in this hall of mirrors. He said that for every student whose parents were able to send them to a therapeutic school to find themselves there were, of course, thousands who did not and could not go. He felt that this "privilege" put great responsibility for the future of a generation on the shoulders of those who had the opportunity to free themselves from this dangerous world.

I have to resist my own inclination to be a latter-day Luddite. My daughters helped me to sign up for Facebook on my sixtieth birthday. Like many in my generation I was a bit nonplussed, wondering how, or whether, I was going to use this new piece of technology. I wasn't entirely sure that I saw the point. After all, I was already equipped with an address book and email that comfortably divided various groups of people in my life. Once up and running I contacted a few people who were likely to be sympathetic about my foray into this new medium and began to worry about how much to reveal and to whom. We all know that all friends are not, in fact, equal. As it turned out, I needn't have worried. Although I now have a sizeable group of "friends," many of these simply constitute people I have met (including several MA alumni) and act as a certain kind of archive. Unlike my daughters, who spend a good deal of time maintaining their Facebook pages and keeping in touch in this way, I find that it has only limited usefulness for me, although I have had a few pleasant encounters with "lost" friends. I am, at this late date in my life, unlikely to use Facebook as a primary mode of communication.

However, many adults are addicted to the tools of this technological age. Some are almost as hard to wean from their smartphones as their children are from video games. One father told me about visiting an old friend in a European city after a five-year absence and being confronted with his surreptitious use of his Blackberry during dinner. He was embarrassed and made the decision never to turn it on during meals again. Another father sent me a copy of a letter he had received from the dean of his distinguished law school. This dean expressed his concern over students who paid more attention in the classroom to their on-line lives than to the lectures and justified his decision to disable wireless connections in the interest of maintaining a competitive law school environment. None of us is immune to the siren call of this virtual world. As adults we expect to be better equipped to deal with these temptations and to check them when they begin to interfere with our day-to-day relationships.

Our children lack this ability. In these young lives technology is now recognized as psyche-changing and identity-shaping. Young people exist in a world of virtual chatter and it is hard for them to find the quiet space to discover who they are and what they think. The bombardment of media and social networking has diminished the uniqueness of the individual voice. We need to monitor those who are not able to monitor themselves and to protect them until they are better able to distinguish fantasy from reality and to develop that "authentic sense of self" to which Raban refers and the skills to handle real relationships. When they have done so, technology will resume its proper place as a tool in their lives, rather than a source of life itself.

We cannot run a school like Montana Academy without access to computers and email, but we are also in a position to control the amount of outside information that our students receive and to turn down the volume of chatter in their lives. We watch with pleasure as they focus on getting to know themselves better and developing close relationships with each other. And we look forward to meeting with you, our parents, face-to-face for three days at our upcoming parent workshop, and to getting to know you better also.

13. DEVELOPING EMPATHY: A LOVE LETTER

FEBRUARY 11, 2010

The subject of empathy was on my mind recently when I read a haunting short reflection called "Night." It was written by Tony Judt, one of my long-time favorite regular commentators in the *New York Review of Books* (January 14, 2010), who turns out to be an exact contemporary of mine and a fellow Cambridge graduate. In this account he describes his experience with Amyotrophic Lateral Sclerosis (ALS)—a motor neuron disorder that gradually imprisons the sentient and still-feeling person within a body that slowly and inexorably ceases to function. Judt's description of this "cockroach-like" existence in which he is utterly and completely dependent on others for a placement of his limbs, a scratch or a minor adjustment is painful to read. After I finished his articulate account of this humiliating helplessness and the ways in which he spends his nights "trussed, myopic and motionless like a modern-day mummy, alone in my corporeal prison, accompanied for the rest of the night only by my thoughts," I had trouble sleeping for several nights. Every time I moved I thought of the impossible task of managing the wish to squirm and being unable to do so. His words had succeeded in evoking in me a close identification with his experience.

What is it that enables us to enter the experience of another person? Not all humans have this capacity. People who suffer from autism cannot do this and those along the "spectrum" with Asperger's syndrome or non-verbal learning disorders struggle to do so. A young child learns to understand the experiences of others via a process we call attunement. A "good enough" parent understands the basic needs of his or her baby, attends to these, and makes the infant feel secure. Combine enough of these experiences and the developing child begins to mirror the care that he has received. We have all watched three- or four-year-old children minister to their baby dolls or stuffed animals. When a parent feels sick or tired and lies down, many young children will come up to take care of him with a tenderness that mimics the care that they themselves have received. And so it goes, ideally, as they grow and begin to have and understand more complex feelings and experiences.

How do our students learn empathy? On campus we make a conscious effort to help them with this task. Many of the students who arrive at Montana Academy are blunted in their development of this achievement, as a consequence of their general immaturity and self-centeredness. The first steps occur, as they do with a young child, in the experience of being understood and cared for themselves before they can accurately understand the needs of others. Gradually we begin to push them beyond their selfish preoccupations to listen to and attune themselves to the experiences of others. When they start to demonstrate that they are able to do this the results are often moving. The daily groups are designed to push them to think about the experience of their fellow students. At first this may be merely an identification: so-and-so feels just like me. John jokes that incoming students tend to exercise their new-found ability to express their feelings and then begin to think about how others might respond to and think about *me*, still lacking the ability to move beyond a fixation on themselves. Eventually, however, a shift starts to take place as relationships deepen. Students begin to see that although there are commonalities, there are also differences, and that each person is unique with respect to their history and experiences. Empathy starts with caring for another and maybe even beginning to see them as equal to oneself in importance. We also ask our students to begin to recognize their parents as separate from themselves, as adults with their own needs and wishes, and to assess how their parents might feel. This journey is a precursor to an adult version of love.

Our Western culture emphasizes the individual to the detriment of the larger social unit, which many other cultures do not do. Whether empathy is more or less developed in other cultures I do not know, but I do think that our society's preoccupation with the individual has made it more difficult for young people to grasp the experience of being part of a social network. On campus we spend a good deal of time helping students to see themselves as contributing members of a small community with its own rules and expectations. Such lessons take place on teams, where students must work together to do chores and relate to each other in groups, and in the dorms where they must learn to live together and cannot avoid being affected by the behavior of others. In the larger community they learn that they can participate and try out new roles during their time at MA.

Above all else, I submit that empathy is learned not through lectures but through close relationships that are formed with other students and with staff. There are few more eloquent demonstrations of this than the goodbye circles held whenever students are leaving campus. Typically these groups follow this format: the students who are staying each address the member of the group that is leaving and then the departing member addresses each remaining individual in the group, including the staff. Just before our December graduation I attended one such goodbye circle for students whom I had come to know well on campus. I was touched by the recognition of struggles between students, their acknowledgement of their own anxieties, false posturing and true feelings. They spoke honestly of regrets about time wasted in fights and misunderstandings, as well as of close times spent in each others' company. They showed genuine affection and shed tears. They expressed admiration for those who had become strong role models for them and were now leaving.

One young man was in tears for five minutes before he could bring himself to speak to his mentor who was leaving. He said that he had been angry with him that very morning when his mentor said to him, "You are my responsibility. Come with me and don't worry about what the others are doing." When he recovered from his anger he realized that he had been reminded of his mother who had often said similar things to him, and admitted how much he would miss the affection and safety of this parallel relationship. As I listened I knew that these young men were well on their way to being caring sons and attentive boyfriends who would eventually step into adult roles as loving husbands and self-sacrificing fathers and strong members of their communities. I was proud of them.

It is no accident that I have been particularly preoccupied with this theme over the past few weeks. Perhaps I should explain. Some of you are aware that my husband, John, had surgery on his neck to relieve spinal stenosis in late October. He recovered well but it became clear after Christmas that he was having a great deal of pain when standing or walking. He returned to the MRI scanner, which revealed a similar stenosis in his lower back. He endured a second long surgery to correct this problem on February 2, and although he is walking much better already, he is still on heavy doses of pain medication. There is nothing quite like watching the suffering of someone you love to remind you of their importance in your life. I want to thank those of you who have sent kind thoughts to both of us and to tell you also that I have appreciated the many expressed concerns from your sons and daughters who have been sweetly solicitous during this time.

14. MY VALENTINE

FEBRUARY 14, 2008

One of the questions that comes up routinely during visits from prospective parents is how we manage co-ed living on campus. Parents are invariably curious, concerned, and want to understand how we handle romantic relationships among our students. The answer is never short and always entails a historical perspective.

There was a time during our first two or three years when this problem preoccupied us on a daily basis. Students eluded staff regularly to brush with each other like hummingbirds on the fly. We found a temporary and partial solution to this problem when we moved the girls' living quarters seven miles off campus to the bottom of Lost Prairie Road where they were housed on what is now Lost Trail Ranch. Even then we joked with each other that seven miles was barely far enough! When that ranch was sold we bought trailers and moved the girls' community back to campus where they were installed in their current location a quarter of a mile from the main campus. During this time our staff were forever vigilant, but male-female boundaries were still breached with a fair degree of regularity.

Around five years ago, we separated the two campuses completely except for the hours spent in the classroom and waited for the students to clamor to be allowed to be back together. There was no such outcry. The girls seemed content, enjoyed their time together, and made it clear that they preferred to have sports time without the boys. The boys stopped preening. Gradually we reintroduced some co-ed time, but we also kept much of the separateness as well. Girls and boys still eat breakfast in different locations and have their morning meetings downstairs and upstairs in the lodge respectively. Most sports take place within the single-gender team structure and staff carefully monitor co-ed time. There are always those who test the limits, but this testing is generally confined to notes and stolen kisses. When staff notice that a student is becoming preoccupied with a particular loved one and failing to pay proper attention to boundaries, they rein in that student and, if he or she fails to heed the warning or defies it, a ten-foot ban is imposed for as long as necessary.

Over time, and with an increase in staff diligence and in clarity about the structure, a different culture has emerged. The boys have begun to treat the girls with respect and the girls have begun to insist on this. One young man very much in love recently talked with me about the upcoming departure of his girlfriend from campus. He confessed that this was his first "true love" and that he was very tempted to break boundaries, an act that he full well acknowledged would produce gratification but would ruin her plans to leave. I was reminded, speaking with him, of an earlier age in which young men and women were trained to put their desires on hold in the interests of education, marriage and family.

Somewhat to the surprise of us all, new students entering Montana Academy now enter a civilized society in which boys and girls treat each other with old-fashioned courtesy. This is a culture controlled by adults and protected from the ramped-up sexual messages that flood the airways via music and television. And it has seemed to us, as we tone down the amplification of sexually explicit media content and set clear expectations for their behavior, that our students experience a sense of relief from sexual expectations and pressures that are both overwhelming and confusing to them. Our experience raises questions about what "adolescence" really is and should be as young people begin to integrate their sexual awareness and the demands of a civilized society.

Montana Academy culture does not fail to present opportunities for romance and these are, for some, a major developmental achievement that gives pleasure to us all. I believe that there is a heightened eroticism in the imposed delay of gratification that more nearly resembles the pre-war era than the promiscuous free-for-all of the long-lingering 60s. Over the years, the culture at Montana Academy has returned to one of relative innocence in which young men and women learn to get to know each other and to explore the possibilities of relationships before throwing themselves at one another. Boys are often seen outside the lower level of the lodge after the morning meeting, waiting to walk to school with a special girl. Couples can be seen talking earnestly in the lodge after meals. Love is alive and well at Montana Academy.

This week the student council arranged a showing of "Casablanca" in the lounge in honor of Valentine's Day, and in April we hold a prom for all students who are at Sun Clan and above.[21] This annual event is held at the Fire Hall in Marion. Student council decorates the hall, and Dave Wagner orchestrates the music and the special dinner. The boys rent tuxes in Kalispell and the girls shop for dresses within a budget of $100. They make their own corsages and look radiant. The staff dress up to join them and the dancing is fun and often flamboyant. John Santa gets out on the dance floor and breaks up couples who are at risk of getting too excited, and even those girls and boys who would otherwise suffer the humiliation of being wallflowers at such events find themselves among friends who understand their social difficulties, love them anyway and make sure that they are included. It is a night to remember.

---

21 Sun Clan is the third of five levels and is generally attained after six or seven months in the program.

15. CHEATING

MARCH 2009

n January I visited an old friend who is an English teacher at a prestigious girls' high school in Dallas. She had just caught a girl in her senior class plagiarizing an essay and had turned her in to the administration. It turned out that this girl was the fourth generation member of her family to attend this school and she had already been charged with cheating in her sophomore year. My friend was agonizing about the appropriate action to take in this situation. She did not feel good about the administration dismissing this girl in her senior year, but worried that she needed to be taught a lesson and knew that the reputation of her school would be at stake if the girl were to pass on without a significant disciplinary action. She wanted her to grow up and accept accountability for her behavior but was unsure about how best to accomplish this. Such conflicts are routine in high-performing schools throughout the country.

The University of Montana has a Center for Ethics. I learned this while listening to our local public radio station, on which the director of this center, Dane Scott, reads an essay once a month on a matter bearing on the subject of ethics. Over a year ago now I found myself listening carefully to what Scott had to say about cheating.

First Scott looked at the statistics. Dr. Donald McCabe of Rutgers University has studied a well-documented national trend that shows increasing rates of cheating among both high school and college students. Scott also quotes a Duke University study that found that seventy-five percent of high school students admitted to cheating, as well as a Stanford University professor who states that "eighty percent of [high school] honors students cheat on a regular basis." Apparently most of these students rarely get caught and, of these, few are punished. If this is the case, Scott asks, "What can we say to these high-achieving young people who feel that in order to be successful they must cheat, especially when they have no fear of getting caught or suffering the consequences?"

Robert Kohlberg has been studying stages of moral development in children for years. When toddlers encounter the world of "no," they are naturally frustrated and have to deal with the fact that ignoring their parents' reprimands can result in punishment. This withdrawal of parental affection or more concrete punishment begins to shape their behavior into socially acceptable channels. By grade school children begin acquiring the ability to delay gratification sufficiently enough that they are willing to respond to reward for desirable behaviors. And by high school we expect that adolescents will have internalized social mores and be motivated both by fear of punishment and wish for reward to avoid behavior that they consciously know to be wrong. Enter the peer group, and the family's ability to shape individual behavior begins to wane. Anyone who has brought up children knows the overwhelming power of the larger culture. The peer group asserts a new and powerful influence over the behavior of the individual. And it appears that in our current adolescent culture there is little to no prohibition against cheating. What power do we, as adults, have to change the peer culture?

Parents and other respected adults can and do raise questions about integrity. We talk about the impact of such behavior on the individual's relationships to her family and friends, on how they will perceive her. We note that a person of integrity is one who can be trusted to be consistent in his responses. Without this demonstration of an internal moral compass a person will behave opportunistically, cannot be relied upon, and will lose the respect of others.

Unless this message is reinforced by the community at large it falls on deaf ears. At Montana Academy we make these matters of character central to our academic and therapeutic curriculum. A few years ago one of our brightest students plagiarized an assignment for an essay because she was lazy and in a hurry. Her teacher, with whom she had been very close, expressed her serious disappointment, as did her parents and therapist. We made a big issue of this lapse and sent her around to every class to speak of her disgrace and to tell others what she had learned from it. I don't think that she will forget the lesson of facing her community, ashamed of her behavior. Besides that, her mother, an academic, has written a book on the subject of plagiarism!

Other schools are working to change the peer culture by promoting a culture of honesty. A *New York Times* article on this subject in October 2008 notes that Dr. Jason Stephens of the University of Connecticut has embarked on a three-year pilot program to reduce cheating in selected high schools by promoting honesty and integrity as habits with positive values throughout life.

Politicians have begun to weigh in on similar social issues. During his campaign, President Obama spoke eloquently about the "deficit of empathy" in the US. In my home country, Great Britain, David Cameron has begun to speak about personal responsibility. Last year he spoke at a by-election lunch in Glasgow where he said that he saw a society that was "in danger of losing its sense of personal responsibility, social responsibility, common decency and yes, even public morality." These powerful adult role models can make a difference in setting a higher standard and this can only begin to help us all to renew a culture of respect and honesty where cheating will be censured and not tolerated.

16. READING HOUR

SEPTEMBER 16, 2008

Around a year ago, I was cozily in bed reading the *London Times Book Review* when I came across an article called "The Uncommon Reader," which caused me to laugh out loud. Alan Bennett's conceit is that the Queen of England has followed her roaming dogs and stumbled across the City of Westminster traveling library van. She wanders off from this encounter with a book in hand and page by page, book by book, becomes a reader. Much to the consternation of her staff and her husband, Prince Philip, the Queen begins to inflict her interest in reading not only on her subjects—abandoning her usual inquires as to length of service, distance traveled, or place of origin—and embarks on a new conversational gambit, "What are you reading at the moment?" At state banquets she leans toward, let's say, the president of France to say, "I've been longing to ask you about the writer Jean Genet." This article has since been turned into a short novella, now available in the US, and I will not spoil it for you by saying any more.

"The Uncommon Reader" was published in 2007 at the same time that the National Endowment for the Arts (NEA) released its report on the decline of reading for pleasure. Several authors were moved to comment on this phenomenon. Ursula Le Guin wrote an article entitled "Staying Awake: Notes on the alleged decline of reading" in the February 2008 edition of *Harpers Magazine*, and Caleb Crain published an article, "Twilight of the Books: What will life be like if people stop reading?" in the *New Yorker* (December 24 & 31, 2007).

Le Guin questions the assumption that books are on their way out and asserts that they are here to stay. She labels 1850-1950 the Century of the Book, in which literacy filtered downward, not only as the front door to individual economic and class advancement, but also as an important social activity and bond. TV shows and sports teams have largely replaced books as common vehicles for social bonding, however Le Guin points to the *Harry Potter* phenomenon as offering both adolescents and young adults an exclusive in-group and shared social experience. She registers the fact that books offer a different form of entertainment from TV (all it needs is light, a human eye, and a human mind) in that "reading is active, an act of attention, of absorbed alertness—not all that different from hunting, or from gathering.... It won't do the work for you. To read a story well is to follow it, to act it, to feel it, to become it—everything short of writing it, in fact.... No wonder not everybody is up to it."

I made a cursory inspection of the boys' dorm bookshelves to find out what they were reading. Certainly there were a good many copies of *Harry Potter,* along with Hemingway, Steinbeck and Cormac McCarthy. But some of the shelves revealed reading tastes that were voracious and far ranging. One such bookshelf contained the following: Peter Robb's *Death in Brazil,* Jim Marrs' *Crossfire: The Plot that Killed Kennedy,* Dan Brown's *Bury My Heart at Wounded Knee,* Machiavelli's *Prince,* Aldous Huxley's *Doors of Perception* and *Heaven and Hell,* the Dalai Lama's *Little Book of Wisdom,* Tom Wolfe's *Bonfire of the Vanities,* Gabriel Garcia Marquez's *One Hundred Years of Solitude,* and, last but not least, *The Ultimate Book of Sports Lists.* Reading is alive and well at Montana Academy. Our students are unquestionably "up to it." Like the Queen, whether purposefully or accidentally, Montana Academy students are readers.

Why is this the case? Certainly our students are bright and, thanks to their parents, they have a wide knowledge of world affairs. And at Carol Santa's insistence, from the very beginning we have set aside a daily Reading Hour. Carol's idea was that this time should be used for self-selected reading for pleasure. She was adamant that unless we structured this time, reading would not take place and that it was important that we protect this time from the pressure of reading for school assignments. This early decision has done much to foster a culture of reading at Montana Academy.

Why is this important? Crain writes in his *New Yorker* article "Twilight of the Books" that "Americans are losing not just the will to read but even the ability." He goes on to suggest that "if, over time, many people choose television over books, then a nation's conversation with itself is likely to change."

He quotes some experimental psychologists as suggesting that a reader and a viewer think differently and speculates that we are at risk of returning to a society of "secondary orality," akin to the primary orality that existed before the emergence of text. The difference between those who are literate and those who are orally based is that literate people can rotate concepts in their minds abstractly. Fluent readers are able to integrate more of their own thoughts and feelings into their experience. Orally oriented people, on the other hand, embed their thoughts in stories and have greater difficulty distancing themselves from electronic technology, so they have trouble negotiating differences of opinion and may be less likely to spend time with ideas that they disagree with. Crain's final line is a warning: "Such a habit might be quite dangerous for a democracy to lose." All of this is provocative, especially in light of our upcoming election.

Although it is fascinating to speculate about where our society is headed, we also continue to focus closer to home on the skills that our students are learning, whether they be for use in the classroom or for pleasure in years to come. In addition to substantial reading, both academic and recreational, we work hard to teach students writing skills in all areas of the curriculum. We include parents when we are able to do so. Jason Rasco runs a yearly class on a selection of Pulitzer Prize-winning authors and is always happy to hear from parents who wish to read along and participate in discussions with students. Some of you already send books to your sons and daughters and talk about them in your weekly phone calls and letters. We welcome you to join in the conversation as part of an extended reading community.

17. SEE NO EVIL

Just before Christmas national news was focused on a report issued by George Mitchell on the subject of the use of performance-enhancing drugs by athletes, particularly baseball players. Mitchell managed to call both athletes and coaches on their unethical behavior and to bring to light many suspected abuses that had previously been hinted at and then vociferously denied. Now there was no denying the serious infiltration of drugs into the world of sports, and disclaimers rang hollow. Mitchell had exposed their behavior and the bubble of general denial was finally punctured.

The sports public has, of course, been part of the problem. They participated in a tacit pact to overlook the drug use of their idols in exchange for the excitement of a great game and the shattering of old records. Coaches, too, were implicated. They themselves were injecting their players in the hopes of enhancing their performance for their mutual self-aggrandizement. Who knows whether or not Mitchell's report will bring about the needed changes, but there is some reason to hope that he has set the stage for this possibility.

This is a familiar scenario to us. Many parents have overlooked their teenage children's use of drugs as long as their children were continuing to do well in school. It is easy to rationalize this position, noting that most teenagers use pot recreationally on weekends, and many also go on to fine colleges where they continue to use drugs discretely with friends. Some manage less well. Many well-respected colleges are plagued with serious alcohol and drug abuse. Anyone who has not read Tom Wolfe's book *I Am Charlotte Simmons* should use this opportunity to wake up to the frightening excesses of contemporary college life.

Many of us parents are children of the sixties and seventies who performed our own experiments with drug use and survived to tell the tale. Parents are generally even more permissive about alcohol use. Most take pleasure in fine wines and reasonable, but also at times excessive, use of hard liquor. We are aware that many European cultures allow children to drink wine with the family at meals, they are not nearly as legally restrictive in their use of alcohol, and this has not necessarily produced a people whose drinking is out of control. Here in America we cannot avoid mixing drinking and driving as easily as Europeans, and our laws are far more stringent. We compromise with our children by teaching them to choose a designated driver who will stay sober at parties. Or we invite their friends to drink safely at home where parents can take hold of car keys if necessary. We tell ourselves that we are teaching them to drink responsibly. Often we are more or less successful with this strategy.

However, I have come to think that we have deceived both ourselves and our children with this approach. What have we really taught them? We have run the risk that the lesson we teach is that we and they are above the law and that we can find ways around laws that don't meet our personal needs or make sense to us. We have demonstrated a double standard by looking the other way so long as things are going well in other respects.

Most of you who have students at Montana Academy have seen the "see no evil" strategy go awry. Some of our teenagers are incapable of drinking responsibly. They are not sipping fine vintages. Many instead have found solace for their troubles in uninhibited use of alcohol. They have led double lives, using and dealing drugs while pretending all is well until the two sides of this fraud collide disastrously.

Such a collision brings sadness and recriminations. Parents can usefully do some soul searching at these times. We should wonder about the impact of our own behavior. While this breast-beating may be inevitable when our children get into trouble, it is only useful if we are truly prepared to make changes. That is harder. At times change may mean acknowledging that the approach itself was faulty. Yet these ingrained class and cultural assumptions are hard to alter. We are likely to resist, much as the sports world will also resist the findings of the Mitchell report. We hope that the scandal will blow over, that we will not really have to make any fundamental changes in our own behavior.

Last winter we had a drug scandal on campus. A few students bought Benadryl when they were on pass with their parents, smuggled it back onto the ranch and shared it with their friends. Some students found the courage to blow the whistle on this subterranean culture. We closed the campus, sent the smugglers back to wilderness, put the campus on "freeze" from normal activities, got down on our hands and knees and searched every inch for contraband. We held marathon groups until we were certain that everyone had taken public accountability for their actions and until it was clear that the adults had recovered control. Gradually a collaborative staff and student culture reasserted itself. The common memory remained mindful of the consequences of these subversive actions for a considerable period of time.

The culture of honesty and responsible sobriety must be sustained by adults. It is time for us to reassert our intolerance of double standards, to rein in our own excesses in support of the attempts that we are asking our children to make to manage their own struggles with both drug and alcohol use. To do so we must look squarely in the mirror and take full account of our wish to look the other way.

18. COFFEE HOUSES AND COMPETENCIES

JUNE 2, 2009

Just prior to our May 15 graduation, the student council put on a coffee house. They rearranged the lodge furniture, set up a stage in the area of the window facing the pond, and manned the kitchen to produce ice cream and cakes. The jazz band was the first to perform, now quite accomplished, having played together for several months under the tutelage of Deidre Corson. Others sang and played in groups of twos and more, with and without accompaniment. One young woman modestly played a successful classical viola piece and another quite new student gave a rousing bongo drum performance. Several staff joined in with their guitars and significant vocal talent. Some students came to the stage willingly. Others were dragged there by their friends. One boy and girl set the house on fire with a skilled display of swing dancing.

These coffee houses have been a feature of life at the ranch for some years now, occurring roughly once every block. They are regularly enjoyed by students and staff. I recall one such event a year ago in January when the snow was blowing hard outside. Inside the lodge the theme was Hawaiian. The student council members were decked out in leis, shades, sailor hats and grass skirts over shorts. A couple of inflatable palm trees graced each side of the stage and there was an island backdrop. Two MCs orchestrated the performers, playing on and off themselves, in many different arrangements and diverse groupings, encouraging and supporting the entire cast from the novice to the accomplished. The mood was one of affectionate tolerance. There was nothing but encouragement for those of lesser talent who had the gumption to get up and give it a try. The staff, as always, generously contributed their own talents in music and dance. I remember, in particular, one student shimmying across the stage in a spontaneous, sinuous grand finale. At the end of it all one of the MCs graciously thanked the student council for all of their hard work and acknowledged the staff talent, reminding his peers that these were not just figures of authority but also people with diverse interests and gifts.

Where did all of this come from? One of the pleasures of founding a school is finding talented staff who take the initiative to create opportunities for students. Dave Wagner, an accomplished guitarist and singer, came to work with us not long after we opened. He was tired of being on the road with his band and, as the staff member responsible for student council, he instituted these regular open-mic events. Deidre Corson, a passionate and multi-talented musician, worked first as weekend staff before heading to the University of Montana to pursue a degree in music education, then returned as our music teacher to create a vibrant musical community at Montana Academy. We are lucky to have them both, and their energetic support of a wide variety of musical opportunities on campus—choir, jazz club, drumming, musicals—has been wonderfully enriching.

Many of our students have talent—some in athletics, some in art, some in academics and some in music and dance. Parents have worked diligently to help them gain competency in their chosen fields. Almost all of these adolescents have had years of exposure to lessons and opportunities, but they have failed ultimately to harness these strengths. They have been missing a core sense of self that would allow them to push themselves forward in any given field and instead they have faltered and drifted. As they resume their development in the structured and simplified world of the ranch community, it is critical that they also have a way to pick up the lost threads of these areas of strength in their lives and to integrate these competencies into their emerging young adult personalities.

Nothing is more demoralizing than inaction. Trauma research has produced an abundance of data to attest to this fact. I recently attended a workshop on trauma by the well-known Boston psychiatrist Bessel Van der Kolk. Dr. Van der Kolk runs the Trauma Center in Brookline, Massachusetts, and has devoted a lifetime of study to this subject. Over and over again he emphasized that trauma resides in the body, that it is not readily accessible to language and that, while we need to create a narrative that helps us to explain and understand what has occurred, the real healing takes place only when "you feel what you feel and know what you know." Darwin first taught us that we all have the same emotions hardwired in us and that the core self carries emotion. We are also fundamentally social creatures. When we are growing up we learn to have friends and to talk about who we are and what we need. At the ranch our daily groups attend to this task.

People who have experienced trauma—and this includes a surprisingly large number of our students—have often lost their way and tried to change their internal sensations via drugs and alcohol. Many have become alienated from their physical selves and lack the capacity to engage pleasurably in the here and now. They need to develop a sense of curiosity about themselves and to reclaim all the scary, needy, disgusting or humiliating parts of themselves. It is our job to help them reinstate a sense of purpose and to remind them that they are the captains of their own ships.

When our students get up on stage in front of their peers to sing or dance or play an instrument, however reluctantly or self-consciously, they are reclaiming a part of themselves, using rhythmic movements and sounds to regulate their emotions and to ground themselves in their bodies. They are once again taking hold of life and finding joy. The coffee houses are beautiful occasions upon which to watch this.

PART III

THE WORLD BEYOND

19. SUCCESS OR FAILURE: WHAT IS AT STAKE?

September 7, 2009

In August, I wrote to you in anticipation of our mid-month graduation exercises. Dr. Malinak was in charge of the ceremony, and he proclaimed his astonishment at the progress that students make while on campus and the transformations that take place before our eyes when our students grow up. He had made his customary visit to the Dollar Store and bought foam hammers as gifts for each graduate, demonstrating to them the need to knock themselves on the head periodically when they make a mistake and to exclaim, "What was I thinking?" in order to remember their time at Montana Academy and to get back to work again. As is our tradition, there were several speeches both by parents joyful to reclaim a child who had been feared lost and by students who wanted to take stock of the distance they had come and the struggles involved, and to acknowledge the support of both the community and their families.

Our many summer visitors have included a good many alumni who have returned while on road trips with their friends to revisit Montana and Montana Academy. These visits bring us great pleasure because they represent the persistence of attachment. These graduates, some recent and some long gone, bring stories of their own transitions to home or college and news of a network of alumni friends with whom they have kept in touch. They are our successes and proof of the efficacy of the work that we do.

Like other therapeutic schools, Montana Academy has been besieged in recent weeks by visiting parents who are anxiously searching the country for the setting in which a failing son or daughter might best begin to thrive and grow. Some debacle has generally punctuated a steady downward slide of 6 to 24 months duration. Sometimes the police have been involved, or a school has expelled the student or simply asked them not to return, or the final report card has been a dismal failure. Sometimes the child has completely stopped going to school, refused to get out of bed and turned nocturnal playing video games. There have been car wrecks and suicide attempts, drug busts and petty theft. Anguished parents have spent sleepless nights staring at the ceiling worrying about how to prop up these failing children and projecting bleak images of a ruined life. Crisis demands action and pushes parents to take the final step of hiring an escort and airlifting a flailing child to safety in the woods. Change is on its way.

Wilderness programs have become skilled at allowing angry and despairing teenagers to howl at the moon until they are ready to sit with their own emotions and begin to want to seek help for themselves. When they are ready to engage, the guide and the group are there to help with the journey toward self-understanding, accountability and reconnection. The transformation begins in the woods. It can be seen in the fresh faces and open smiles in the pictures that parents bring on the next stage of their journey to visit schools. Both parents and students have begun to believe that change is possible and that the future can be bright after all. They have had a taste of success, and hope has once again taken root in their hearts. Perhaps this pain will become a thing of the past and their child will now move forward and resume a normal developmental trajectory.

But wise parents know that stable change cannot sustain itself without a new consistent environment with steady structure and support. They commit to the search for a setting that will promote ongoing internal growth in self-awareness, empathy, adherence to rules, and the ability to make mature relationships and plans for the future.

What if this process fails? And it may. By the time a student arrives at graduation we have lived with them for twelve to twenty-four months and know how they think and whether or not they have grown up. We hope to have done more than keep them safe. We do our best to place both the light and dark cards on the table and not gloss over the struggles that will show up in the months and years after graduation. We generally know those who may return to using drugs, those who are likely to struggle in school, and those who will either collapse back into their families or distance themselves from them.

Recently we had bad news from several alumni families. One mother wrote to us about her daughter's wretched life with her boyfriend, also a former student. This young couple had just been turned out of his parents' basement, where they had been living, because the parents could no longer tolerate the drug deals, thefts and squalor of their lives. These young adults had not been able to maintain steady employment or find a decent place to live for more than a few weeks at a time. They had no transportation, were using drugs routinely, and had been robbed twice at gunpoint. Last week another anguished father called to say that he had received a three-a.m. call from an emergency room in another state where his daughter had almost died of a heroin overdose just before she was due to start her junior year of college. A third mother reported that her son lived for two weeks in a raunchy hotel with crack dealers and single moms running away from their boyfriends. This son went to court on his mother's fiftieth birthday for a misdemeanor for alcohol possession. Other stories are less dramatically painful but reflect a continued failure to take hold. Parents worry about their young adult son's repeated inability to finish courses at a junior college, a serious tendency to procrastinate that might unseat an otherwise promising college career, a reemergence of entitlement, and a failure to buckle down and get a summer job.

Parents, too, must begin to learn when to intervene and when to let go. It may make sense to bring out the cavalry and affect a major rescue for a failing sixteen-year-old who needs to sit safely in the woods until he can stop pouting and get on with the tasks of everyday life and learn to take care of himself. But it does not make sense to keep supporting a twenty-two-year-old son who has failed three semesters of college. Nor does it make sense to keep a drug dealer in the basement or pay for college when a daughter is using heroin. The hardest lesson that parents learn is to let go and let life begin to take over the process of teaching. This doesn't mean that parents should stop caring, hoping for the best, or supporting reasonable plans. They need to know that they have done their part, that they have dealt with their own internal demons to the best of their abilities, that they have been open and responsive to their child's needs, provided the best opportunities that they could for growth, and made realistic plans for the future. Then they need to stop cushioning their child against the inevitable struggles ahead, let go, and wish them well.

Montana Academy prides itself on selecting students who are likely to be successful in our milieu, as well as parents who will both stay the course and work on themselves as well as their relationship with their child. We believe that all children are influenced by the attitudes of parents in regard to most things in life, and in treatment, toward their own psychological work. If you are ready to begin this important work for yourselves I suggest that you consider reading *Parenting from the Inside Out*[22] by Daniel Siegel and Mary Hartzell. This will provide a guide for you to work alongside your child toward a better understanding of how your own early experiences may have affected your parenting and how such an understanding can also improve it.

Now that your teenager is safe it is an opportunity to take stock of your own part in the unfolding family drama, to "own your own" as Dr. Malinak likes to say. We will be teaching parents about both recognition and limit setting at the October parent workshops and preparing you to take advantage of this time of growth and healing in the hope that you and your children will be our success stories and not our failures.

A warm welcome to all our new families and to those of you providing ongoing support here for your children.

---

22   Daniel Siegel, MD, and Mary Hartzell, M.ED. *Parenting from the Inside Out.* Jeremy P. New York: Tarcher/ Penguin Group, 2003.

20. PRODIGAL SONS AND DAUGHTERS

MAY 6, 2010

In mid-May, we are getting ready for another graduation in which we honor those students who have worked hard both academically and therapeutically to earn the right to return home. Some will graduate from campus and go home to attend local schools in the fall. Others will graduate from high school and Skyhouse with the promise of college ahead. They will leave the bosom of the Montana Academy family and return home. One graduate told me that she thinks of Montana Academy as a large family with a lot of weird aunts and uncles who she likes but doesn't see very much. I was amused by this vision of what I meant to her and flattered by its intimacy.

I was sitting with a team of boys recently exploring their family roles as victims, clowns and scapegoats when one of them brought up the role of the prodigal son (Luke 15:11–32). Only one student knew the story well and he told his own version, naming the many misdeeds of the son—his squandering of the family's resources on "riotous living," his anger and lying, his dependence on drugs and rejection of his family. When the son finally recovers his senses and is ready to return to the bosom of his family they welcome him with open arms and throw him a large feast, saying to their other son, "Thy brother was dead, and is alive again; and was lost, and is found." All the boys resonated with the story. They were all lost sons and hoped that they would eventually be forgiven and welcomed home. Such is the task of our graduation, a bittersweet leaving and joyful return. Occasionally, however, there is a student who fails to make this important benchmark at the expected time.

One of the most difficult tasks that falls to the leadership of Montana Academy is the firing of a student. Fortunately this is a rare occurrence, but it does happen from time to time and when it does, we all suffer and the whole community shares in the pain. This is, of course, a parent's nightmare.

Students are sent to MA because they are out of control in a variety of ways. We are careful in our selection of students since we are an open campus with access to rocks, trees, ropes and other tools that could be used as weapons for students intent on harming themselves or others. We do not use restraints on campus and we do not have any kind of time-out room, so there are some behaviors that we cannot begin to treat. We rarely accept a student with a history of any violence beyond angry tantrums in which crockery may be smashed and parents shoved. Naturally we expect that students who have exhibited such behavior at home may well demonstrate similar behavior on campus. It is common for us to find that students have punched holes in walls and we make them responsible for fixing these. There is one form of behavior that is unacceptable and that is assault of either a staff member or student. This is virtually an automatic cause for expulsion because it renders the campus unsafe for other students to do their work.

As the whole community knows, such an incident occurred recently at Skyhouse where one of our young men, who had a long history of disregulation of his emotions, lost his temper and threw another student against the wall and punched him until a third student intervened. The fire extinguisher was dislodged in the scuffle and discharged, spraying them all in the face.

The young man in question had spent almost two years in treatment. He had put a good many holes in walls on campus and struggled hard to manage his emotions. He had made significant progress and was attending the local community college, had secured a spot in the college of his choice, and was in his final months of our program. We anguished over the necessity of his departure and were aware that he could well decide to throw away all his gains in treatment and return to his former extensive drug use. His mother was horrified by his actions and our decision. She wrote that she was "stunned, heartbroken, sad and numb." She said that she could strangle her son and wanted to shout the battle cry of Alanon, "After all I've done for you!" In the end she proved herself a self-proclaimed survivor and steadfast parent. Within twenty-four hours she had secured a place for him in a sober living environment where he could also continue his community college courses. His long-time MA therapist promised to stay in touch with him. He will be missed at graduation, and if and when he finally succeeds in gaining self-control, we, too, will welcome his return with open arms.

21. LEARNING ABOUT OTHERS

NOVEMBER 12, 2010

My annual routine is punctuated by the biannual meetings of the Independent Educational Consultants Association, to which boarding schools and therapeutic programs are also invited. I have just returned from Cincinnati where I encountered many old friends, met some interesting potential new colleagues and attended presentations on adopted teenagers, current treatments of bipolar and co-morbid disorders, and innovative approaches to eating disorders.

Earlier this year John and I attended meetings in Toronto where he gave several professional presentations and we both spent time with consultants. One consultant teased me by giving an amusing imitation of my attempts to turn down students that she wished to send to Montana Academy. She had discovered that if she could just find some foreign angle to intrigue me then perhaps I might be willing to take a second look at a particular case and even find an extra space.

Toronto is one of the most diverse cities in North America. Kalispell is one of the least, and the sight of an obvious foreigner walking down Main Street there is enough to turn heads. Montana itself is an almost exclusively white state with strong ties to Garrison Keiler's world of dutiful Lutherans and Catholics who celebrate their various Scandinavian heritages and where animal clubs and the Sons of Norway provide local gathering places. At its worst it also exemplifies a small-town, Sarah Palin, parochial world view that clings to its right to bear arms, form militias and fight "big government." A frightening CBS video, *The Fire Next Time*, took a look at this strongly anti-environmentalist side of Kalispell in 2002. While this aspect of Montana undoubtedly exists and is currently exemplified by an Aryan nation group that is attempting to create a base here, it is undercut by newer, more liberal forces. Kalispell held its first gay pride parade in 2009 and only a few Bible-toting fanatics turned up to fulminate.

Our students have created their own unusual community in northwest Montana. Here on our remote campus they have gathered from all parts of the country, joined by a few outliers from the larger world. While they are in flight from various troubles of modern life, with which they have been afflicted and from which they require asylum to cure, they have not forgotten the rest of the world. It filters through to them without the intrusion of constant media and they have time to reflect and be moved by it. Certainly the Haitian earthquake touched them deeply and they took it upon themselves to raise money to help its victims both by organizing a campus community day with various activities and by designing and selling T-shirts at the spring parent workshop. More recently our students took up the cause of child soldiers in Uganda, and at our October parent workshop one father showed a clip from a film that he had made on this subject. Our students designed and sold "Invisible Children" T-shirts as a benefit for this group. Over our academic pause in mid-February a student also arranged a series of TED[23] talks on a wide variety of subjects in which both students and staff participated. I was present at one such talk by Emmanuel Jal, a child soldier from southern Sudan whose family had been killed and who had been raised to hate Arabs and Muslims. He was rescued by a young British woman, Emma McCune, who educated him and introduced him to the wider world where he has risen beyond his personal traumas and uses music to reach out against racial and religious hatred. It would have been easy to hear a pin drop in that classroom. In the discussion that followed, everyone wanted to share their thoughts about trauma and forgiveness, their own sense of privilege, their admiration of Emmanuel's courage and their fear that they would be complacent and forget his plea for action and their own need to give back. One young man, the son of an immigrant from Gaza, spoke of his childhood knee-jerk anger against Israelis and said that he had come to realize through living with many Jewish friends on campus that he needed to rethink his hatred and broaden his knowledge of a complex situation.

---

23   TED is a non-profit devoted to Ideas Worth Spreading, bringing together people from Technology, Entertainment and Design.

Another father, Anan Abu Taleb, gave a talk to the local Middle East forum in Whitefish after the spring parent workshop and several Montana Academy families and staff attended along with students from Skyhouse. Anan spoke of his early traumatic experiences growing up under Israeli occupation in Gaza and about returning there in January to visit his ailing parents and view the 2009 bombed shell of his elementary school where his father had taught for thirty-five years. Yet there was no hatred in his talk, only pain and a plea for peace that would allow everyone to move on to secure the future they wanted for their children. I was reminded of the courage of another Palestinian attorney living in Jerusalem. Elias Khoury chose to turn his pain over two events—his father's death in a Palestinian terrorist attack in 1975 and the more recent murder of his twenty-year-old son, George, also shot by Palestinians who assumed that he was a Jew out for a jog—into an act of cultural healing. Khoury paid for the translation into Arabic of Amos Oz's autobiography, *A Tale of Love and Darkness*.[24] Khoury, like Anan, understood that both sides are immersed in their own tragedies and oblivious to the pain of the other (*New York Times*, March 2010). Today we are enrolling a new student who has grown up in Jerusalem and is likely to add her own experiences to this ongoing dialogue.

Gwynne Hales is right about me. I do want to bring the wider world to Montana Academy and we are, indeed, fortunate to have a number of students with attachments outside the US who help to keep our community focused outward as well as inward. We have also invested in a summer internship program to bring senior or post-graduate students to spend time on campus. Over the years we have had summer interns from several fine American universities and from Italy and Singapore. This summer we hired an agricultural studies intern, a graduate from Clark University who has made three trips to Africa in her young life and who spent last summer in southern Sudan where she and a Dinka friend raised $10,000 to build a solid school. She had wonderful stories to share with our students while they worked together in the garden this summer.

Many students go on from Montana Academy to a gap semester. Three girls who were all on the same team on campus have recently been involved in projects in far-flung corners of the world. One lived and studied in Varanasi,

---

24   Amos Oz. *A Tale of Love and Darkness*. Boston: Houghton Mifflin, 2004.

India. Another worked on a coffee plantation in Costa Rica, and a third worked for five months with vervet monkeys in South Africa. Another young graduate spent the past year at the Hebrew University in Jerusalem and has come back twice during the past year to speak of his experiences there. Several of our December graduates are making plans now to explore the world in the months after they graduate.

I like to think that the experience of these young people in Montana has deepened their sense of community. They have not been allowed to be alone or in front of a screen. They have learned something about themselves, about caring for others and accepting their differences. Experiencing diversity does not just come by making contact with people from other walks of life; it is also learned through a fine attunement to individual differences in whatever form they may take, by seeing beyond the mask and into the heart of another. It is quite possible to travel the world and make little contact with the people in it. Elias Khoury believes that literature can provide a bridge. Our students have learned the value of belonging to a community and of openness to the experience of others. They will take these experiences with them wherever they go next.

22. CELEBRATIONS

DECEMBER 10, 2009

n late September, while our students were out exploring the mountains and woods of Montana, I went back to the flatlands of East Anglia to visit my mother, now in a nursing home, and to help my brother who has been preoccupied for the duration of the summer with her care and the task of moving her belongings out of her home and preparing the house for rental. I spent many hours going through the papers and photos that she had collected over a life spanning more than ninety years—her childhood during "the Troubles" in Northern Ireland and college years spent studying French and German at Queen's University in Belfast, a post-graduate year in Leipzig, Germany just before war broke out, war years in Britain's top secret Bletchley Park, and subsequent years as a diplomat's wife in the Middle East. Amongst her photos were pictures of the baby boy that she gave birth to in Iraq and who is buried there. I had never seen them before. It was a sad and difficult trip in many ways and yet, because it took place in Cambridge, it was also a rich and stimulating one.

Cambridge was celebrating the 800th anniversary of its founding. Its year-long series of events culminated in September with an alumni weekend of lectures and showcasing of college libraries, collections and gardens. Everywhere I went Cambridge was also celebrating a second important anniversary—the 200th anniversary of Charles Darwin's birth. I visited Darwin's rooms at Christ's College, an exhibit at the Sedgewick Museum of his geological interests pursued under Professor Lyell, and another exhibit at the University botanical gardens of his tutelage at the side of the botanist Professor Henslowe. I also attended a newly released film about Darwin's life, *Creation*, which I can recommend for its human portrait of the man behind the ideas. It focuses in particular on Darwin's family life and his close relationship with his firstborn child, Annie, his overwhelming grief when she died at age nine and the ways in which he blamed himself for her death and felt alienated from his wife, Emma Wedgewood, who found consolation in her faith.

Best of all, I spent time at a wonderful exhibit at the Fitzwilliam Museum on Darwin's influence on the visual arts. This may seem a slightly improbable subject, but the exhibit turned out to be a profound portrayal of many of the ways in which Darwin's ideas influenced the artists of his time, particularly the Impressionists like Degas whose reading of his work informed his sculptures of simian-like dancers and Cezanne who ventured afield into the countryside to paint accompanied by a geologist friend who instructed him in fossils and rock formations. Other well-known artists also devoted themselves to studies of geological phenomena. Coming from Montana I was entranced by Thomas Moran's pictures of geothermal springs in Yellowstone and pictures of glaciers and mountain ranges. Still other artists portrayed the animal kingdom, following Darwin's interest in the expression of emotions in animals and humans, natural and sexual selection. The exhibit juxtaposed stunning displays of feathers from the Argus pheasant with an Impressionist portrait of ladies sporting seductive feathers in their fashionable hats. One arresting portrait by Landseer of two stags locked in mortal combat brought me back to thoughts of Montana, where hunting season is a serious annual rite.

Several of our staff take pleasure not merely in the sport but in the task of bringing home a year's supply of meat. Some of them feed their families exclusively on game. Considerable skill is involved in hunting with a bow rather than a gun. A few weekends ago one of our staff went out with his bow and bugled in a big bull elk close to campus where he felled the animal at nine yards. He sent for his wife to bring the horses and help drag out the meat, and she asked if any students would like to take part in this work. Eight Earth Clan boys volunteered. I spoke to them the following Monday morning and it was clear that they had been riveted by the experience of spending four or five hours watching the butchering of a large elk and the careful attempt to use every possible piece of the carcass. A few of them made their own jerky to take on their camping trips. Several weeks later another staff member was called down to the pasture by the horse corral where a deer had broken its hind leg trying to jump a fence. After he shot the wounded animal he called his team down to the pasture for an anatomy lesson as he quartered and dressed the carcass. While he was down at the corral a second deer panicked and rushed the tall fence, where its antlers caught and broke its neck. Another team of boys came down to help with this second field dressing and they donated the resulting meat to the local food bank. For the majority this was exposure to a raw encounter between humans and the animal kingdom.

Who knows what these young people will take away from such experiences. Indeed, we are not certain of what they will choose to make of their experience in this unusual school in the relatively remote terrain of northwest Montana. Darwin failed out of medical school in Edinburgh and his father, who likely worried about him, suggested that he go to Cambridge to pursue a respectable career in the church. Instead he spent his time chasing beetles and going on long walks to talk about geology and botany with Henslowe. When he graduated he was lucky to be recommended for a long sea voyage, as some might pursue a gap year (or three as it turned out for Darwin), and observed everything from the indigenous people of Terra del Fuego to the beaks of finches and much, much more. He gave up on his faith and he did not publish his ideas for over twenty years, but in the end he changed the way we think about the world. The paths in life are infinite, some successful and some not. We are sufficiently saturated with some of Darwin's ideas about natural selection and survival of the species to want to do everything that is in our power to give our offspring the best possible chance of success. We grieve over our children's struggles and blame ourselves for their failures and even their deaths, as Darwin did. At the same time we do know that there is no straight road to life's success or fulfillment.

On December 18, we will once again gather in the warmth of the lodge to enjoy the graduation of a large group of students. Together with their families we will celebrate the overcoming of their struggles, their newfound poise and maturity, and their promise. And then, bittersweet as always, we will say goodbye and return to focus our attention on those who are still with us.

23. GRADUATION—THE LONG VIEW

In mid-May we celebrated our first of two summer graduations, mainly for students leaving Skyhouse. We will shortly be celebrating our second graduation in mid-August for students leaving for college or returning home to finish school. These are times when we recognize the important work that your children have accomplished during their stay at Montana Academy and wish them well on their launch into the next stages of life's journey. This is a time to look forward and consider the longer view.

It so happened that on the very eve of our May graduation I received my monthly copy of *The Atlantic* (June 2009) and began to read an article entitled "What Makes us Happy?" by Joshua Wolf Shenk. This article details the findings of an important longitudinal study, comprised of the Grant and Glueck studies of the Harvard Grant Study of Adult Development, which has interested both John and me over the years. The Grant study, begun in 1937 to follow a group of 268 healthy, well-adjusted Harvard (male) sophomores over the course of their lives, has now been in progress for seventy years. George Vaillant, a psychiatrist, discovered the study in 1967 and began to work with the material that had been gathered around the time of the twenty-fifth college reunion of the group, and has spent his entire career studying these men, as well as material provided as a control group by a study begun in the same time period of juvenile delinquents—the Glueck group. The results of these two life-long studies are instructive and seem to support both the philosophy and the work that we do at Montana Academy.

So, what are their findings? Like us, Valliant is concerned about his subjects' "adaptations" (think "approach") to life's struggles. He looks, as we do, to the work of Anna Freud for understanding human defenses and believes that much of what is labeled as mental illness is a reflection of "unwise" deployment of defense mechanisms. He says, "If we use our defenses well, we are deemed mentally healthy, conscientious, funny, creative and altruistic. If we use them badly, the psychiatrist diagnoses us as ill, our neighbors label us as unpleasant and society brands us as immoral." Vaillant notes four categories of defenses, ranging from the most primitive (paranoia and hallucination) to "immature" (acting out, passive aggression, hypochondria, projection and fantasy) to the common "neurotic" defenses of intellectualization and repression and, last of all, to the healthiest or most "mature" adaptations of altruism, humor, anticipation (looking ahead and planning for future discomfort), suppression (a conscious decision to postpone attention to an impulse or conflict to be addressed in good time) and sublimation (finding outlets for feelings). He notes, as we also do, that immature defenses fade with maturity and that the capacity to employ mature adaptations bodes well for healthy aging, along with education, stable marriages, not smoking, not abusing alcohol, exercise and healthy weight. The single most significant finding of this study is the power of relationships, and Vaillant emphasizes that the only things that really matter in life are relationships to other people. We cannot know what troubles our children are going to face in their lives, but we can seek to fortify them so they can approach life's challenges with the requisite strength of character.

Coincidentally, the same week that I read about Vaillant's study in *The Atlantic*, I also found myself reading an article by Jonah Lehrer in the May 18 issue of the *New Yorker* entitled "Don't." The article discusses the long-term effects of the ability to delay gratification. An ingenious study, "the marshmallow test," is described. Four-year-olds were left alone in a room with a marshmallow for a few minutes and instructed that if they did not eat the marshmallow until the examiner returned they would be given two. A decade later those students who were able to wait fifteen minutes at age four had an SAT score that was, on average, two hundred and ten points higher than those of the children who could wait only thirty seconds! Young children who struggled to delay gratification were noted to struggle in stressful situations as well, often had trouble paying attention and found it difficult to maintain friendships, in addition to achieving lower SAT scores later on.

These extraordinary predictive findings suggest the enormous importance of self-control and raise all kinds of questions about how we best teach our children this essential life skill. This task begins early in life, as the study suggests. I recently read elsewhere that in our society most Americans prefer to accept $50 now to $100 in six months. Like the general population, many of the students at Montana Academy have, for one reason or another, failed to learn the lessons of self-control and patience. Our highly structured environment tries to make up for this failure. We repeatedly insist that students not only wait (for promotions, for privileges, for attention), but also that they work to earn their rewards. Nothing is more gratifying than to hear from parents of our graduates that their students have learned to work hard, to pay their own way, and to understand the value of money and, particularly, of relationships. Two parents who accompanied their alumni students to our May graduation glowed with pleasure at the newfound maturity of their young adult children who were headed to college this fall ready to handle the tasks ahead of them. Two other alumni passed an adolescent "marshmallow" test in the weeks following their graduation in December. They attended a well-known outdoor program and were invited by their fellow participants to smoke a little weed on a mountaintop behind the staff's backs. They declined. In due course, the staff discovered the breaking of the "no drug use" contract by six of the twelve students on the trip. Those six were dismissed in disgrace while our students graduated the program honorably. Small wonder, then, that we have confidence in them for the future. We are all proud parents at such moments.

As we pause on the threshold of our August graduation, we do not know what the future holds for our graduates, how they will be tested, and how they will meet these life tests. I take comfort in the words of the final chapter of George Eliot's *Middlemarch*:

> Every limit is a beginning as well as an ending. Who can quit young lives after being so long in company with them, and not desire to know what befell them in their after-years? For the fragments of a life, however typical, is not the sample of an even web: promises may not be kept, and an ardent outset may be followed by declension;

latent powers may find their long-waited opportunity; a past error may urge a grand retrieval.

So, to graduates and their families, I say please stay in touch. And to those who remain, we still have work to do together.

CPSIA information can be obtained at www.ICGtesting.com
Printed in the USA
BVOW10*2102240813

329349BV00001B/1/P